Power Cut?

POWER CUT?

How the EU Is Pulling the Plug on Electricity Markets

CARLO STAGNARO

Institute of
Economic Affairs

First published in Great Britain in 2015 by
The Institute of Economic Affairs
2 Lord North Street
Westminster
London SW1P 3LB
in association with London Publishing Partnership Ltd
www.londonpublishingpartnership.co.uk

The mission of the Institute of Economic Affairs is to improve understanding of the fundamental institutions of a free society by analysing and expounding the role of markets in solving economic and social problems.

A CIP catalogue record for this book is available from the British Library.

ISBN 978-0-255-36716-5

Many IEA publications are translated into languages other than English or are reprinted. Permission to translate or to reprint should be sought from the Director General at the address above.

Typeset in Kepler by T&T Productions Ltd
www.tandtproductions.com

Printed and bound in Great Britain by Hobbs the Printers Ltd

CONTENTS

THE AUTHOR

Carlo Stagnaro is Senior Fellow of Istituto Bruno Leoni, of which he was Research and Studies Director until April 2014. He currently heads the technical secretariat of Italy's Minister of Economic Development, Ms Federica Guidi. After graduating in Environmental Engineering at the University of Genoa, he achieved a PhD in Economics, Markets and Institutions from IMT Alti Studi Lucca. His research interests are in the fields of energy economics, public service economics, and liberalisation and privatisation processes. His Twitter account is @CarloStagnaro. The ideas and opinions expressed in this monograph belong to the author alone, and do not necessarily reflect those of the institutions with which he may work or cooperate.

FOREWORD

In the United Kingdom, polls regularly suggest that a majority of people support a renationalisation of the energy companies. This is despite the huge success of the programme of privatisation and liberalisation that saw prices falling rapidly as competition was promoted. Not only did prices fall but, between 1990 and 2010, greenhouse gas emissions per unit of GDP fell by 45 per cent.

In recent years, though, there have been problems; but those problems can hardly be blamed on privatisation. Competition has been restricted as a matter of deliberate policy. Furthermore, measures to reduce carbon emissions have been introduced that are incredibly inefficient in the sense that they are designed to achieve their goal in a very expensive way. The way in which 'green' energy sources have been promoted has led to much greater regulation of the industry and a return to the policy of the government 'picking winners' – that is, deciding how much to subsidise electricity produced using different technologies. The intermittency of many renewable energy sources then leads to efforts by regulators to ensure that there is spare capacity in the system.

At one time, the UK was a leading light in Europe when it came to energy liberalisation. To some extent, the European Union wished to follow the UK's lead. However, EU regulation has made liberalisation and competition much more difficult. There has been some increase in competition: dominant nationalised firms have faced challenges from electricity producers in other countries. But the attempts by the EU to promote competition and liberalisation have been only an intermittent success.

This is partly because the EU lacks the power to promote a pro-liberalisation and pro-privatisation agenda. It is also because the EU has less enthusiasm for the project than the British government had in the 1980s. Moreover, the EU is implementing forms of regulation designed to promote renewables that are incompatible with genuine competition. Indeed, some aspects of the re-regulation of the UK market have happened as a result of EU directives.

EU and UK energy policies lead to much higher levels of carbon emissions for a given cost than is necessary, less security of supply, higher prices and less competition. The unsatisfactory results of regulation lead to yet more regulation.

Energy expert Carlo Stagnaro demonstrates the folly of EU and UK policy in relation to electricity markets in this important book. He also shows that there is an alternative. Even if the government wishes to put a price on carbon emissions and promote the objective of reducing emissions, this could be done using much better policies than the ones currently directed to that end. It is possible to have a liberalised, competitive energy market in which energy is delivered at lower cost. Furthermore, for those who believe that the reduction in carbon dioxide emissions is an absolute priority, such a liberalised market would reduce emissions at a much lower cost or, alternatively, produce much lower emissions for a given cost. By favouring central planning over a competitive market, policymakers are actually undermining the achievement of a major objective at the heart of policy.

Carlo Stagnaro sets out a policy agenda for the EU that also has important lessons for the UK. It deserves to be taken seriously by all who have an interest in a well-functioning energy market.

The views expressed in this monograph are, as in all IEA publications, those of the authors and not those of the Institute (which has no corporate view), its managing trustees, Academic Advisory Council members or senior staff. With some exceptions, such as with the publication of lectures, all IEA monographs are blind peer-reviewed by at least two academics or researchers who are experts in the field.

PHILIP BOOTH
Editorial and Programme Director
Institute of Economic Affairs
Professor of Finance, Public Policy and Ethics
St Mary's University, Twickenham

October 2015

ACKNOWLEDGMENT

I wish to thank a few friends who were kind enough to comment upon previous versions of this monograph, or parts thereof: Simona Benedettini, Rosamaria Bitetti, David Henderson, Alberto Mingardi, Massimo Nicolazzi, Federico Testa and Stefano Verde. A special thanks goes to Alberto Cló – who is more than a friend and a mentor – not just for his comments but also for all that he tried to teach me. I am also grateful to Philip Booth for his encouragement, assistance and advice, and to the IEA for having accepted this book for publication.

I would also like to thank Edoardo Battisti, Alberto Biancardi, Vito Cozzoli, Franco Debenedetti, Oscar Giannino, Lynne Kiesling, Luciano Lavecchia, Stephen Littlechild, Alfredo Macchiati, Marlene Melpignano, David Perazzoni, Giovanni Piccirilli, Salvatore Rebecchini, Massimo Ricci, Colin Robinson, Enrico Romagna Manoja, Silvio Schinaia, Serena Sileoni, Chicco Testa, Ilian Vassilev, George Yarrow and many others. Discussing with them and reading their writings on energy and competition issues has been truly enriching.

I am particularly grateful to two anonymous referees, who reviewed the first draft and helped me to better focus and streamline my argument.

It would be unfair not to thank my colleagues at Istituto Bruno Leoni and at Italy's Ministry for Economic Development for tolerating all the time I took off to work on this book. This applies to Silvana, Andrea Giovanni and Anna Rosa even more so.

Last, but not least, a truly special mention goes to Federica Guidi, both for the large degree of freedom that she left me, and for giving me the unique opportunity to study the Beast from the inside and get involved in the electricity market liberalisation process in Italy.

The usual disclaimer applies.

SUMMARY

- Technical features of the electricity industry, together with the ideological climate that prevailed after World War II, led to nationalisation. Over time, it became clear that the arguments for nationalisation were unconvincing. Firstly, changes in technology led to the ability to produce electricity on a smaller scale. Secondly, it became clear that, even if some parts of the process of electricity production and distribution had 'natural monopoly' aspects, other parts did not. Moreover, it became increasingly understood that state electricity suppliers were very inefficient.

- The UK led the way when it came to reform. Markets were deregulated, competition was promoted and the industry was privatised. There was then price-cap regulation of the natural monopoly element. From 1990 to 1999, electricity charges for domestic consumers fell by 26 per cent, with a larger fall for industrial users. Electricity companies were able to use cheaper fuels, free from political constraints. It was not only energy prices that fell in the UK after liberalisation; energy-related greenhouse gas emissions fell by 12 per cent between 1990 and 2010, and emissions per unit of GDP fell by 45 per cent.

- There have been a number of attempts, through EU directives that followed the British model to some extent, to liberalise electricity markets in the EU more generally. By 2007, all EU member states had third-party access (TPA) to electricity networks, and most had transparent wholesale markets and a degree of consumer choice. As a result, the average

market share of incumbent dominant firms in the EU fell
from 64.9 per cent in 1999 to 55.9 per cent in 2010. Several
private and foreign companies also entered markets that had
previously been state monopolies. However, these steps were
also accompanied by harmonisation and centralisation of
regulation at the EU level.

• Around ten years ago, there began a major policy U-turn in
the UK. Steps that have reduced competition and the degree
of liberalisation include limiting the number of offers and
tariffs that suppliers can make to residential consumers,
measures that direct electricity generating companies
towards particular technologies and long-term agreements
to fix prices in markets (such as the agreement with the
Chinese government in relation to nuclear energy that
guarantees a price about twice the current wholesale price
of electricity). These measures will crowd out non-subsidised
investments in which the taxpayer does not bear the risk.

• The British U-turn was paralleled by a push from the EU
as well as member states towards interventionist climate
policies. For example, there are often capital subsidies or
tax breaks to install renewable capacity, direct subsidies for
renewable energy and feed-in tariffs, which treat renewable
generation very favourably. In addition, member states
have to grant either priority access or guaranteed access
to the grid for 'green' electricity. These policies have many
detrimental effects. For example, when the demand for
electricity falls – as it did post-2008 – renewable energy
producers are immune to the consequences. Also, subsidies
vary hugely across different technologies and different
countries. Photovoltaics received an average subsidy of €496/
MWh in the Czech Republic and slightly lower subsidies in
Belgium, France, Italy and Luxembourg, whereas biogas
and waste received an average subsidy of only €2.76/MWh
in Finland. This causes enormous market distortion. To put

it simply, for a given cost, the reduction in carbon emissions has been much smaller than if more economically rational mechanisms had been used.

- The cost of reducing CO_2 outputs has been huge under EU policies. Even in Finland – the country that has been able to reduce CO_2 emissions most cheaply – the cost per tonne of reduced carbon emissions has been around three to five times the value of permits under the EU emissions trading scheme, which provides a proxy for the cost of achieving the decarbonisation goals efficiently. In France, the marginal cost could be around 50 times higher than in Finland. This arises because the compulsory use of national renewables targets means that countries such as Sweden and France are replacing generating capacity that emits very little carbon with renewables. This is hugely wasteful. A carbon tax or cap-and-trade system alone would lead to a much more efficient outcome.

- Further problems caused by climate change policies include the genuinely competitive part of the market being reduced in size and significant supply-and-demand imbalances. Also, the intermittency inherent in many renewable sources of energy leads to price spikes and the potential for either huge increases in consumer prices or blackouts.

- Intermittency has led to pressure for regulated capacity support mechanisms – yet another intervention in the market. These reduce competition further by remunerating electricity producers in a highly regulated environment. Producers are rewarded not for actually producing and distributing power, but for simply having the capacity to do so. Regulatory intervention in this area is not necessary. Where there is the potential for intermittency, market processes are needed to discover whether consumers prefer energy markets to be subject to price spikes and intermittent supply, or whether they prefer a higher average price and more reliable supply and price patterns. Different consumers may have different preferences that can be provided by different companies or tariffs.

- Whilst the latest EU climate change policy may prove to be less expensive than its predecessor, we are a long way from liberalised and efficient energy markets in which CO_2 emissions are reduced in the cheapest possible way.
- The UK needs to return to, and the EU to develop, a fully liberalised and competitive energy market. Even if policymakers believe they cannot rely on free markets to correctly price negative externalities from carbon emissions, they should devise policies that supplement markets in internalising the environmental costs of energy production and consumption patterns. This should be combined with liberalisation and the promotion of competition and innovation, both at the wholesale and retail level. The UK experience between 1990 and 2005 showed how successful such policies can be.

TABLES, FIGURES AND BOXES

1 INTRODUCTION

Electricity is a defining mark – possibly *the* defining mark – of modern societies. Try a little thought experiment. Imagine that you travel into the past with a time machine. As you step out of it, you do not know into which era you have moved; you are just in the middle of nowhere. You look around. It may be very hard to tell whether you are, for example, in Roman times, or in the Middle Ages. But if you see electric lights everywhere around you, there can be no doubt: you are in the twentieth century or later. The revolution of electricity has been so deep, wide and pervasive that, as economic historian Vaclav Smil (2005: 13) argues:

> [T]his was the first advance in nearly 4.5 billion years of the planet's evolution that led to the generation of cosmically detectable signals of intelligent life on Earth: a new civilisation was born, one based on synergy of scientific advances, technical innovation, aggressive commercialization, and intensifying, and increasingly efficient, conversions of energy.

Electricity is ubiquitous in our societies. And, of course, electricity is the fundamental input of our digital societies: without electricity, there would be no smartphones, computers, internet and so on.

To put it in the most straightforward way, electricity is so simple to use and so widespread – at least in the developed world, but to a growing extent in the developing world too – that we

1

take it for granted. We can survive one or more days if natural gas is cut off, or if it is not possible to find petrol for our cars; perhaps we can even deal with water being cut off for some time. But if electricity were unavailable for a prolonged period of time, we would be nearly paralysed. In fact, the notion that one billion or more people worldwide lack reliable access to electricity is perceived as a serious problem. Energy poverty is one of the main challenges our world must face. Access to reliable, cheap energy is the key to prosperity (Goklany 2007).

The production and delivery of electrical power is, however, complex – and it is especially complex for the consumer to understand its production and delivery. The best definition for it was possibly provided by a non-scientist, singer Ray Charles:

> Soul [music] is when you take a song and make it a part of you – a part that's so true, so real, people think it must have happened to you ... It's like electricity – we don't really know what it is, do we? But it's a force that can light a room. Soul is like electricity, like a spirit, a drive, a power.

In a way, this quotation can be reversed: electricity is like soul. A relevant feature of electricity is that it is not a *thing* – a good that you may or may not own. Electricity is a physical phenomenon, which is due to the flow of electrons (actually, a *wave* of electrons) through a conductor. Every material is, to some extent, a conductor, but some materials are better than others. In fact, some materials are such bad conductors that we use them for the opposite task – that is, to isolate things from electricity.

Most people, however, are not interested in the physics of electricity. They have never heard of Gustav R. Kirchhoff or Georg Ohm, after whom are named the fundamental laws that govern electricity flow through circuits. People simply want the current to flow when they push a button. And, of course, people want cheap energy that is easily accessible.

Complex supply chains and state monopolies

In order to have cheap, reliable electricity, there has to be a complex supply chain. Each segment of the supply chain requires large investments and very specific know-how. Firstly, electricity must be generated. Primary sources of energy such as coal, oil, natural gas, solar radiation, wind, etc., must be found, and technologies need to be deployed that can transform them into electricity. Then electricity needs to be moved from the place where it is generated to the place where it is to be consumed. Electricity moves through networks, and, given the present state of technology, it cannot be economically stored on a large scale. Transmission networks operate over long distances; distribution networks are designed to deliver electricity to end consumers. There is no difference, in principle, between transmission and distribution infrastructure, except that the former is high voltage and the latter is low voltage. Finally, electricity must be measured (metered) and consumed.

The electricity industry is heavily regulated. In most countries, and for most of the 'age of electricity', there has been no market at all for electricity. It has been provided by vertically integrated, state monopolies, only subject to political control rather than to economic incentives – though there are important exceptions to this general rule.

Tackling environmental concerns

Even when and where the monopoly is broken up, regulations still dictate a number of details related to how electricity should be produced, dispatched, consumed and priced. The EU, for example, has promoted a number of environmental policies aimed at reducing carbon emissions. The most relevant of such policies is hugely subsidising renewable energy sources, particularly solar and wind power. The technical and economic problems created by renewables (especially their intermittency) are being addressed in a way that further reduces the scope of competition in power markets. The central thesis of this book is that EU climate policies have jeopardised competitive energy markets. It is also argued that, from a purely environmental point of view, green subsidies are both ineffective and inefficient. Finally, it is argued that the environmental goal of cutting carbon emissions may well be achieved (and to some extent has been achieved) by relying on competitive markets, which may be complemented by technology-neutral environmental policies. Regulations are often badly designed, and, while aiming at a specific target (for example, low prices or high reliability), they result in a number of undesirable consequences, such as scarcity or lower levels of technological innovation (Van den Bergh and Pacces 2010).

Environmental regulations (particularly those relating to decarbonisation) have a major impact on how electricity is generated, exchanged and consumed. Below we examine whether the EU has the most effective and efficient carbon-reduction policies, assuming that such policies are appropriate. We also consider how the EU's climate policies interact with the (mostly) liberalised framework that has been developed for the electricity industry.

Summary

This book is divided into five parts. The first part considers the theoretical framework that is adopted to analyse the regulation of electricity markets, the impact of regulation on the industry's organisation and the relevant externalities that regulation is often developed to address. The most important of such externalities is climate change, and the most relevant policies in the EU are those aimed at reducing carbon emissions and promoting renewables and other carbon-free sources of energy.

The second part details the EU legal framework that is related to electricity and climate regulation. It shows that the former has by and large followed the example set by the UK with its policy of privatisation and liberalisation, even though some defining features of that model are missing in the EU directives. As far as climate regulation is concerned, however, the EU has taken a much more interventionist stance, though its aims are not always clear, and environmental goals and policy tools are mixed with old-style 'industrial policies'.

The third part looks at the interaction of liberalisation policies with climate policies, and argues that they inevitably come to contradict one another. This endangers European liberalisation and explains the anti-liberalisation backlash in Great Britain. In other words, if electricity liberalisation is pursued consistently, it will make it harder for the EU to meet its environmental goals through the policy instruments it has adopted. More specifically, EU climate policies have introduced a number of distortions in electricity markets that need to be tackled.

The fourth part looks at those distortions and envisages two possible approaches, which are developed in the fifth part. One approach sets as a priority the maintenance of current environmental policies and implies more government intervention and centralisation of electricity markets. The other, which is market oriented, requires the EU's environmental policies to be fundamentally revised – even if its goals are not revised. Policies would have to change at the national level too, as many nation states – including the UK – operate policies that are more distortionary than EU climate policies ought to be.

At the time of writing, there are confusing messages both at the EU and national level. On the one hand, there are signs of a shift towards a more market-friendly approach; on the other hand, there are also signs of a governmental backlash. This may be the most crucial time for the future of Europe's energy policies since the 1980s. Choices that are being made now may be irreversible in the short-to-medium run. If market-oriented policies are implemented, the EU has a chance to develop well-functioning markets that also make it possible to achieve environmental goals. If, on the contrary, the push back to state control prevails, the ghost of the past – when electricity systems were plagued with inefficiencies and risks were socialised – may be back haunting Europe.

PART 1

THE THEORETICAL FRAMEWORK

The curious task of economics is to demonstrate to men how little they really know about what they imagine they can design. To the naive mind that can conceive of order only as the product of deliberate arrangement, it may seem absurd that in complex conditions order, and adaptation to the unknown, can be achieved more effectively by decentralizing decisions and that a division of authority will actually extend the possibility of overall order. Yet that decentralization actually leads to more information being taken into account.

Friedrich Hayek (1988: 76)

2 THE CLIMATE–ENERGY NEXUS

Carbon emissions and energy

Most of the energy we consume comes from fossil fuels, such as coal, oil and natural gas. For example, the EU's gross inland consumption was as much as 1,665 Mtoe (million tonnes of oil equivalent) in 2013. Of this, 73 per cent came from fossil fuels (Figure 1).

Fossil fuels are used because they are either cheaper or more efficient (or both) compared with alternatives (Epstein 2014; Smil 2010, 2014). Unfortunately, the process of burning fossil fuels generates a number of by-products. Some of these are pollutants, though energy-producing and energy-consuming technologies are regulated in order to maintain such pollutants below the

Figure 1   EU28's gross inland consumption of energy by source (2013, left panel) and gross electricity generation by source (2013, right panel)

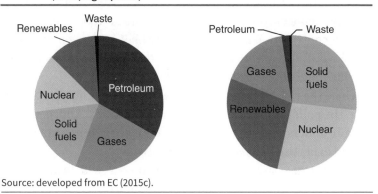

Source: developed from EC (2015c).

thresholds that are believed to be safe for human health and the environment. Not only regulation, but also – and possibly foremost – market forces promote the adoption of cleaner technologies as they become available (Anderson and Leal 2001).

'Traditional' pollutants, such as particulates, NO_x and SO_x, cause rapid and localised harm: for example, particulates are correlated with serious illnesses, such as lung cancer and an increase in cardiopulmonary mortality. Other by-products act in a more subtle way. This is the case with carbon dioxide (CO_2) and other so-called greenhouse gases (GHGs), such as methane (CH_4), ozone (O_3) and water vapour (H_2O). GHGs are suspected of contributing to a potentially dangerous increase in the planet's average temperature (IPCC 2007, 2013).

The physics and economics of climate change are both very complex issues, and a broad debate among experts is ongoing (Bradley 2004; Helm 2012; Nordhaus 2008; Robinson 2008). According to the Intergovernmental Panel on Climate Change (IPCC) – an intergovernmental body in charge of collecting climate science and making it available for governments in order to improve their ability to make sound policy decisions – if warming exceeds 2 °C above pre-industrial levels, adverse impacts may be severe. If warming exceeds 4 °C, the consequences may even be catastrophic. Therefore, the IPCC has called on the international community to take action and reduce GHGs to a level such that their concentration in the atmosphere is stabilised, and the human contribution to climate change becomes acceptable. It is not the purpose of this book to dispute these claims, which are outside the author's area of expertise.

Once the risk of man-made global warming is accepted, however, the policy implications are far from obvious. And, it should be said, understanding policy trade-offs is something outside the area of expertise of most climate scientists.

Some argue that economic development will bring about technological innovation, and that technology will solve the problem. After all, climate change does not happen overnight: it is a slow process, and it is both impossible and wrong to try and solve it in the short run. Humanity does have time, and it may be better to delay making expensive decisions. Economic freedom also increases wealth and makes available the resources needed to cope with the effects of climate change. If this is correct, promoting economic freedom worldwide may be the best way to deal with this issue (Goklany 2007; Montgomery and Tuladhar 2006; Simon 1996).

Others believe that economic freedom, and perhaps even economic development, is not enough, or that it does not help at all. They suggest that policies are implemented in order to internalise the 'social' or 'external' costs arising from burning fossil fuels. Several alternative policies may be adopted in order to achieve the result, but there are significant underlying uncertainties. Since global warming is a global phenomenon, a first-best solution might be to implement these policies at a global level. For several reasons, it has not been possible so far – and it will hardly be possible in the future (Helm 2012) – to meet this goal. The Kyoto Protocol, which is the closest thing to a global treaty that we have had, only committed a limited set of countries to cut their own GHG emissions by a small amount (5.2 per cent).

Within such a framework, the EU took unilateral action. In 2007, a commitment was made to cut emissions by 20 per cent below 1990 levels by 2020, and to cover 20 per cent of final energy consumption with renewable energy sources (RES) by the same deadline. This package of policies is known as 20-20-20. Further commitments are being made in the longer run, including setting a very ambitious (and, in the author's view, quite unrealistic) goal of achieving an almost full decarbonisation of the economy by 2050. An intermediate goal – cutting European emissions by 40 per cent by 2030 – was proposed by the European Council during its meeting of 23–24 October 2014.

An obvious criticism of EU policies is that global warming is a global phenomenon, and it is emissions at a global level that matter. If you only cut emissions within a region, it may make little difference. In fact, an unintended result may be achieved: if the effort to cut emissions drives energy prices to such a level that energy-intensive industries move to lower cost jurisdictions where more carbon-intensive technologies are used, global emissions might actually increase. This phenomenon is known as 'carbon leakage', and the EU is trying to deal with it by regulating it.

Though global attempts to reduce carbon emissions have not been successful, reducing them is not an entirely EU effort. Other countries, such as New Zealand, and several US states are implementing policies to control emissions. Even developing countries have declared that they share a similar objective. China in particular made a joint commitment with the US to set a carbon target for 2030, although this commitment may require just a small deviation from their baseline carbon emissions, unlike the significant cuts proposed by the EU (Bronson and Levy 2014). So far, however, global, coordinated action is still missing.

The EU's commitment to cutting emissions led to the adoption of several directives and regulations that affect the way energy is produced and consumed. Electricity accounts for about 22 per cent of the entire amount of energy consumed annually in the EU (EC 2014a). For this reason alone, it is a target for those who wish to impose environmental policies such as those described above. Low- or zero-carbon electricity generation processes already exist and, in some cases, are economically viable. For example, natural gas-fuelled plants emit on average half as much carbon as coal-fuelled plants, and renewable and nuclear energy do not emit carbon at all. It also happens to be the case that the enforcement of environmental regulations is easier in relation to electricity generation because its production tends to be concentrated and large scale.

In most of this book, the issue of whether climate policies are needed will not be discussed. We will also not discuss whether it is better to set a short- or medium-run, quantitative target – as the EU did – than to focus on more long-term trends. It will be taken as given that carbon emissions will be reduced and that regulations will be introduced to achieve this objective. The focus of the discussion below will be on the kind of regulations that have been introduced in the EU, with particular regard to renewables subsidies and mandates, and their impact on electricity market design, structure and competition.

Are climate change policies inconsistent with broadly free markets?

There is no reason, in principle, for climate policies to be inconsistent with competitive electricity markets. In practice, however, the way in which climate policies are implemented is damaging to electricity markets. Indeed, it is argued in this book that the EU is doing much harm both to markets and the climate by implementing policies that are scarcely coordinated with each other, that very often counteract each other and, to a large extent, that are driven by rent-seeking interests.

In particular, two broad approaches to climate policy may be identified. One approach is market based, and the other relies more on discretionary political decision-making. Carbon taxes and cap-and-trade schemes (see Box 1) that are designed to be technology neutral belong to the former category. They place a competitive advantage on 'clean(er)' sources, which is proportional to the alleged environmental benefit they produce (i.e. to the avoided emissions).

Other policies to reduce carbon emissions are much more distortionary. This is the case with mandates and subsidies. These policies also tend to reduce competition in energy markets for three reasons.

Box 1   Carbon taxes versus cap-and-trade schemes

Carbon taxes and cap-and-trade schemes are both market-based tools to reduce emissions. They differ from command-and-control and other, more interventionist policies insofar as the ultimate decisions are left to market participants. Of course, political decision makers determine by how much carbon output should be reduced – there is planning at that level – but not how it should be reduced.

The difference between taxes and cap-and-trade schemes lies in the fact that a carbon tax puts a price on the emissions and leaves it up to market participants to adjust the quantities; hence, a carbon tax incorporates a 'marginal social cost' into the market price of the production of electricity. Under a cap-and-trade scheme, scarcity is artificially created in the production of the emissions, and market agents will discover the price of creating an externality by trading the right to emit. While a carbon tax and a cap-and-trade scheme are equivalent in principle, they differ from the point of view of the underlying uncertainties. In a world free of transaction costs, carbon taxes and cap-and-trade schemes are equivalent; i.e. the optimal carbon tax would reduce emissions down to a level that is equal to the cap of the optimal cap-and-trade scheme, and vice versa.

(a) A given market share is 'segregated' from the usual supply-and-demand interactions because producing technologies are picked by virtue of regulatory decisions, even though they may not be the most efficient ones.

(b) As far as that 'segregated' or 'non-contestable' part of the market is concerned, the price mechanism is to some extent shut off. Prices are set by regulators in a way that

The choice between a carbon tax and a cap-and-trade scheme depends on a number of considerations, which range from their political feasibility via the nature of the underlying uncertainties to the kind of transaction costs that are involved (Nordhaus 2008; Weitzman 1974; Hepburn 2006). Either policy can (and does) have several shortcomings, yet they have only an indirect effect on electricity markets. They change the market agents' choices by changing the relative prices of different technologies and ensuring that the output of carbon emissions under the various technologies is seen as a cost. However, they do not determine such choices. Producers can use the cheapest technology, given the cost in terms of carbon emissions that the technologies generate. In short, carbon taxes and cap-and-trade are consistent with a framework in which the fundamental choices regarding energy production and consumption are decentralised and left to market agents.

does not necessarily reflect either the opportunity cost of specific technologies or the marginal social benefit derived from lower emissions.

(c) For technical reasons, some of the most heavily subsidised sources of energy in the EU (such as solar panels and wind turbines) result in intermittent generation; i.e. their production profile cannot be programmed insofar as it depends on an external, unknown (or little known) input (sun or wind). This generates large costs in the system and further distorts the way competition works, as will be discussed in later chapters.

The presence of a large amount of subsidised generating capacity producing intermittent supply also raises a number of technical problems, which tend to be addressed through regulatory provisions. One such example is capacity support schemes, which are designed to ensure that enough spare capacity is available to back up intermittent energy sources when they are not sufficient to meet demand.

3 ELECTRICITY – FROM POWER STATION TO HOUSEHOLD

Some of the economic problems within electricity markets arise because of the engineering and physical practicalities of electricity generation. It is therefore worth considering these issues briefly. Electrical systems are made of three main components: generation facilities, transmission and distribution networks.

Generators transform some form of primary energy – typically, the chemical energy incorporated in fossil fuels, or the potential energy provided by the height gap between the generator and a water basin, the kinetic energy of the wind or the sun's radiation – into electricity. With the notable exception of solar power, the basic technology is the same for most generators: a turbine is made to rotate by a force acting upon it. The force may arise from steam from the combustion of fossil fuels, or from the flow of water or wind. The turbine's shaft will rotate, together with a coil of copper wire that is attached to it (the armature). On either side of the armature are placed magnets. A law of physics – known as Faraday's law of induction – states that, if a wire conductor rotates within a magnetic field, an electric current is generated that may be retrieved and shipped outside the generator. The basic technology, despite all the improvements that have been made over time, is still the same as it was in the late nineteenth century (Smil 2005).

The electricity industry as we know it is the result of a complex story (Bodanis 2005), in which physical, technical, economic, regulatory and commercial challenges have been addressed over time. At any point in time, however, the industry has been subject to a number of technical constraints. Two are most relevant to this book. Firstly, the electricity system as a whole must always be kept in real-time equilibrium: imbalances between demand and supply may result in a failure of the system itself (a blackout). Secondly, given the present state of technology, electricity cannot be stored in a cost-effective way. Significant progress has been made in the development of ever-more efficient batteries and other storage technologies, but, at present, there seems to be no silver bullet (Hadjipaschalis et al. 2009).

The ability to prevent blackouts and other systemic shocks depends on a number of variables, including the available technology, the degree of coordination within the system, the supply- and demand-side responses and the underlying institutional arrangements (Giberson and Kiesling 2004).

Power systems

From a technical point of view, an electrical system is like a transmission chain. At one end, a generator produces electricity, which is moved first through high-voltage transmission lines and then through low-voltage distribution wires. It is eventually consumed at the opposite end of the system by the final user. Figure 2 shows a typical electricity system.

A greater penetration of renewable energy sources arising from either subsidies or genuine improvements in efficiency may change the transmission and distribution mechanisms significantly. Traditional energy sources, such as coal and nuclear power, tend to show significant economies of scale. Therefore, electricity systems tend to grow around a small number of large generating plants. Most renewables, however, tend to be deployed on a small scale and permit more decentralised generation. Some of them tend also to be non-programmable: the output of a wind

Figure 2 Transmission and distribution grids within the power industry

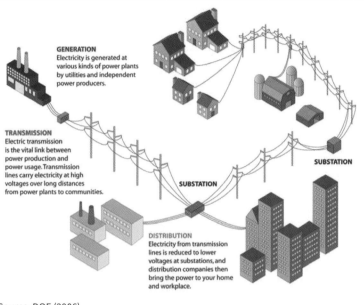

GENERATION
Electricity is generated at various kinds of power plants by utilities and independent power producers.

TRANSMISSION
Electric transmission is the vital link between power production and power usage. Transmission lines carry electricity at high voltages over long distances from power plants to communities.

SUBSTATION

SUBSTATION

DISTRIBUTION
Electricity from transmission lines is reduced to lower voltages at substations, and distribution companies then bring the power to your home and workplace.

Source: DOE (2006).

or solar plant depends on an exogenous input (wind or sun) that cannot be controlled, albeit it can be approximately forecasted. This makes the development of storage technologies much more important.

The use of non-programmable renewables has a significant influence on how systems are organised. Overproduction can happen when demand is low (for example, if wind blows at night). Production can also suddenly skyrocket or collapse (for example, as clouds come and go). As electrical intermittency – the load produced by intermittent generators – increases, the challenge of keeping the entire network in real-time equilibrium becomes more difficult and costly. The challenge is both technical and economic. How do we deal with intermittency? And how do we find the cheapest way to achieve this goal? When choosing between renewables and choosing between renewable and non-renewable sources of electricity, intermittency and the cost of dealing with it has to be factored in to the decision-making process.

Another way of asking the same question leads to the central issues that we cover below: what kind of institutional arrangements (see Box 2) may fit best with the need to provide consumers with cheap, reliable and sustainable electricity? How, where and under what conditions can competition be brought into play? Such goals require a high degree of coordination among different 'pieces' of the system: how can this best be achieved? What is the appropriate role (if any) for government? What is meant by a 'market' for electricity?

Box 2　Institutions matter

The behaviour of economic actors is strongly dependent on the incentives they face. Such behaviour, in turn, leads to outcomes that each of us may deem as more or less desirable. The role of institutions has been underestimated for a long time; thereafter, it has been often misunderstood. According to Sala-i-Martin (2002: 18), the term 'institutions' may be used to refer to 'various aspects of law enforcement ... the functioning of markets ... inequality and social conflicts ... political institutions ... the health system ... financial institutions ... as well as government institutions.' North (1991: 97) explained that 'institutions are the humanly devised constraints that structure political, economic, and social interactions. They consist of both informal constraints (sanctions, taboos, customs, traditions and codes of conduct), and formal rules (constitutions, laws, property rights).'

To be effective, institutions need to display two characteristics. Firstly, they should make it possible to achieve the
goals that are regarded as socially desirable. Secondly, they
should be able to deal with changing conditions. The more
able institutions are to adapt to changes, the more they tend
to be resilient over time.

Transactions between economic agents must occur, and
such transactions have a cost. The costs can involve the need
to look for information (which may not be readily or easily
available) about the goods being traded and/or the people
who may want to sell or buy them, the costs of contracting,
the incomplete nature of virtually any contract and so on.
Without transaction costs, institutions are almost irrelevant,
as is the initial distribution of property rights. This is a major
finding of Coase (1960) (see also Forte 2007). However, transaction costs are ubiquitous. If they are too high, transactions
may not happen. Good (or bad) institutions may drive transaction costs downwards (or upwards). This is why institutional
design – as well as institutional experimentation and evolution – is so important. It requires a great deal of attention to
the unintended consequences of institutional choices. Such
consequences can include, but are not limited to, induced
rigidities, lost opportunities, inefficient behaviours and an
impact on the organisation and the size of firms.

4 THE NATURAL MONOPOLY PROBLEM IN ELECTRICITY

In the beginning, the electricity industry was unregulated. As time passed, however, it became heavily regulated, partly because the ideological pendulum swung towards state intervention, partly because of technological constraints (Zorzoli 2011) and partly because incumbents viewed regulation as a tool to protect their profits from competitors (Kiesling 2008; Smil 2005, 2010). Economic historians may well find in this story a powerful example of what Krueger (1974) called 'rent-seeking society'.

The entire industry became regulated at an early stage under the belief that it was a natural monopoly (see Box 3). Even if it is questionable that regulation delivered more benefits than costs, there was a rationale for regulation. Some parts of the industry really were natural monopolies. It is absurd even to think about competing transmission or distribution networks, at least in the most densely populated areas of Europe and North America where the power industry developed first, given the then-existing state of technology. The cost of duplication from having several sets of cables connecting producers with consumers would be immense. In addition, especially several decades ago, a small number of plants – if not just one – were enough to serve an entire city. There were significant economies of scale. Therefore, generation was also considered a natural monopoly. There were also significant economies of scale in metering and billing. At the same time, the intellectual case against utility regulation still had to be developed (Demsetz 1968). All of these factors led to regulation, and this was followed by state ownership. Coordination between the different parts of the production chain was also a major problem. A vertically integrated industry, where information could easily move up or down the chain (thus reducing transactions costs), seemed like a rational approach. Once the idea was accepted that electricity would inherently become a vertically integrated monopoly, the step towards state ownership was very small in most jurisdictions.

It is difficult to know – even in retrospect – whether a monopoly was the most efficient corporate structure for the electricity industry, or whether this structure arose as a result of lobbying activities from incumbents as well as government intervention and nationalisation. We do not have the counterfactual. Certainly, it was attuned to the intellectual climate of the time to treat the industry as a natural monopoly. In these circumstances, it is no surprise that almost everywhere in the world, and everywhere in Europe, the industry eventually fell into the hands of the state.

Has technological progress killed the 'natural monopoly' argument?

Several things happened over time that had a bearing on the natural monopoly argument for regulating electricity (Kiesling 2008). As transmission (and voltage transformation) technologies improved, it became possible and economical to move electricity over longer distances. The alleged 'natural monopoly' nature of generation, which meant that it was believed that you needed a single generator close to a population centre, became less and less credible. It became efficient for many generators to fuel many cities at the same time. In this way, each power plant could be used in the most efficient way, and – more relevant to our analysis – plants became able to compete against each other. Such an efficiency gain was critically dependent on an interconnected

Box 3   The natural monopoly problem

A natural monopoly will tend to arise when the production costs of a single firm supplying the entire market are lower than those of two or more firms competing with each other. This is characterised by the marginal cost of additional output steeply declining as output increases, both in the short run and in the long run. A natural monopoly is also defined by the mathematical property of the subadditivity of costs. Typically, natural monopolies arise when fixed costs are very large compared with variable costs.

A natural monopoly poses a major problem. Mainstream economic theory calls for government to prevent the monopolist from using its market power to restrict output and raise prices. The nature of government intervention may vary depending on the characteristics of the industry. Intervention may take the form of command and control, state ownership, price regulation or a combination of these things.

It is not always efficient to regulate a natural monopoly. Sometimes, the costs of regulation can be higher than the social cost of the monopolist operating to maximise profits. This may happen, for example, when the cost of enforcement

transmission network being available to transmit the electricity produced by different generators. There may still have been a natural monopoly within the market, but it existed – if at all – in a more narrowly defined area of the industry.

The recording and storing of information then became easier, as did metering consumption. Individual billing also became more economic. Eventually, the development of information and communications technology made it increasingly possible to treat different pieces of the system as separate industries, rather is high or, more subtly, when regulation (especially price regulation) prevents investment and technological developments that might, in the long run, turn a supposedly natural monopoly into a competitive industry. This may be true in the case of electricity. A seminal paper by Posner (1969) showed that, because a natural monopoly's very existence can be due to technological barriers, progress may dismantle them. As such, governments should be very careful in deciding how to regulate, and whether they should regulate, an industry.

Identifying natural monopolies is far more complex in practice than in theory, and successive intellectual waves change the situation faced by a potential regulator. Joskow (2007) summarises as follows: '[t]he pendulum of policy toward real and imagined natural monopoly problems has swung from limited regulation, to a dramatic expansion of regulation, to a gradual return to a more limited scope for price and entry regulation.' The crucial point is whether costs of regulation are higher or lower than the costs of the monopoly itself – a question that, more often than not, seems to find an answer that is very critical of government intervention (Carlton and Peltzman 2010).

than one vertically integrated industry. Coordination among different stages of the value chain became possible. There was a change in the intellectual climate too. Visionaries imagined that competition might deliver benefits that decades of state monopoly had neglected. As the first institutional experiments were made, a growing number of scholars agreed that the natural monopoly issue was, by and large, no longer an absolute constraint. In particular, it became clear that generation could be liberalised, and wholesale and retail markets could be introduced.

The fact that it became technologically feasible and possibly cost-effective to move away from the old state-controlled monopoly systems was a necessary condition for change, but it was not a sufficient condition. In the absence of an intellectual and political consensus, institutional changes would not have happened. However, this consensus developed for various reasons. Firstly, decades of state ownership had led to overinvestment in capital assets as well as to the kind of inefficiencies that are very often associated with public monopolies (Considine and Kleit 2007). There were cost overruns and poor service, and little attention was given to the consumer. Power companies employed an excessive number of strongly unionised workers and often made losses. The power system, instead of growing along a sustainable path, soon became plagued by a disproportionate amount of fixed, sunk costs. The pricing mechanism – which, in most places, was designed as a sort of 'cost-plus' scheme whereby costs are entirely passed down to consumers – was very inefficient. It discouraged innovation because companies could not capture the benefits of innovation and did not perceive the cost of inefficient structures, whose burden was passed down to end users in a monopolised system with entirely captive consumers.

Technological progress, institutional evolution and a growing understanding of the underlying economics drove a dramatic change of the intellectual and policy climate.

5 MARKET CLEARING AND THE PROBLEM OF RENEWABLES

Regulation can be justified for the part of the electricity industry that could be described as a natural monopoly. However, the rest of the industry can operate in the same market institutional framework as other businesses: in other words, it can be fully liberalised. This includes generation, power-trading and retail markets. In principle, electricity is a bundle of different services, some of which may be entirely deregulated, while others are subject to forms of regulation. Following Stoft (2002), such services can be divided in five groups.

- Ancillary services that are needed to ensure the system is kept in balance at any time: these have public good characteristics and are also subject to externalities. Such systems are usually fully regulated on the demand side so that the likelihood of power 'outages' is low, but they may be deregulated on the supply side so that providers can compete against each other.

- Unit commitment and congestion management:[1] traditionally, a 'system operator' would be in charge of these issues. As time passes, it becomes increasingly possible to leave it up to the market to perform at least part of these

---

1   For any given level of demand a decision must be made about which generating units will produce the required energy. Potential congestion must also be managed, whether due to insufficient network capacity or to unforeseen faults.

tasks, but the system operator may still need to have a last word on many aspects.

- Risk management and forward markets: both generators and consumers are risk averse. The creation of forward markets may provide the tools to manage both upside and downside risks in the most efficient way.

- Transmission and distribution: this is the quintessential natural monopoly within the power sector, but even here there is room to grow for market transactions and competition. However, by and large, if any part of the system needs to be regulated, it is the transmission and distribution function.

- Retail competition: there is a great deal of resistance to full liberalisation at the retail level as a result of concerns that weak customers – especially households and small businesses – would not be able to make the most efficient choices. Nevertheless, competition is possible and beneficial (Kiesling 2007; Rassenti et al. 2002; Riezner and Testa 2003).

In terms of market design, the most crucial parts are the wholesale markets and balancing tools that ensure that supply and demand are in equilibrium, together with retail markets. Many renewables have an impact on prices for the end consumer and they may distort risk distribution. However, subsidised intermittent power, such as wind, has a much larger impact on the market actors' behaviour.

How the electricity market clears

Generally speaking, the electricity market is organised according to different time horizons. The most important market is the 'day-ahead market'. It is usually closed one day in advance of the physical delivery of power, and it provides guidance to generators and the system operator as to how much power should be produced and from where it will be obtained.

Day-ahead markets define the wholesale price of electricity. They are usually organised as 'double auctions', though this may vary. Generally speaking, 'asks' (prices at which generators are willing to sell) and 'bids' (prices at which consumers are willing to buy) are made with regard to one-hour intervals. Generators submit their ask prices, and these are put in ascending order to build a supply curve. Bids are put in descending order to build a demand curve. The supply and demand curves will meet at a point that corresponds to the price that clears the market. In most power markets, a 'system marginal price rule' holds, under which each generator who asks for a lower price than the clearing one is awarded the market-clearing price. This means that the market-clearing price is equal to the marginal cost of generation, i.e. the cost of the last unit of energy that is produced. The last generator will earn zero profits, while other generators will earn profits that are equal to the difference between the market-clearing price and their own marginal costs. These profits (often called inframarginal rents) should be high enough in normal circumstances to not only ensure that fixed, sunk costs can be recovered but also provide an incentive to invest in new capacity when the expected future demand is higher than the theoretical generation capacity. The list of generators, from the lowest to the highest asked prices, is called the 'merit order curve'.

Figure 3 shows a typical supply-and-demand curve in a power market. In this case, a large number of generators ask for a price equal to zero. This may be because producers are using renewables with zero marginal cost of production, or because they manage 'baseload' plants with very low marginal costs. This can be the case with nuclear power, for which shut-on–shut-off cycles take a very long time, during which the plant keeps producing power. Once a threshold level is reached, more, higher priced generators come into play, and the asked price rises very sharply. As far as the demand curve is concerned, the first piece of it is very

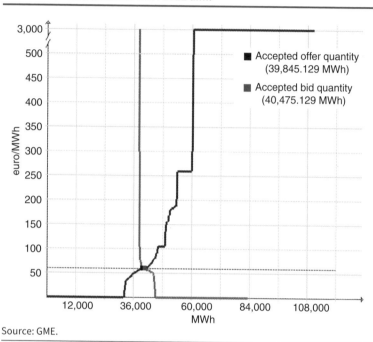

Figure 3 Supply and demand curves in the Italian Power Exchange (IPEX) on 10 December 2014 at 12 a.m.

■ Accepted offer quantity (39,845.129 MWh)

■ Accepted bid quantity (40,475.129 MWh)

Source: GME.

rigid. Everything from hospitals and industrial plants to refrigerators and other appliances need to run at virtually any cost. Thereafter, agents on the demand side become more responsive to price signals. Eventually, a price of around 61 euro/MWh clears the market in this case. Figure 3 refers to a typical working day (10 December 2014) between 12 p.m. and 1 p.m. in Italy.

For several reasons, however, the demanded quantities may be different from those expected. For example, if a day is warmer (or colder) than expected, power demand may fall (or rise). Or an industrial facility may find itself with more or less production to perform at a given time on a given day. In this case, both sellers and buyers have a chance to adjust their positions as well as the opportunity to do so in one or more further market session(s). But even this may not be enough to maintain the system in equilibrium. Sudden, unforeseen changes may occur either on the demand or on the supply side. On the supply side, this may happen because of intermittent facilities in the case of wind and solar energy, or because of a production fault in a conventional plant. On the demand side, it may happen for reasons as mundane as intervals in extremely popular televised events leading to surges in demand when people make tea. For example, the UK's National Grid predicted a pick-up of around 3,000 MW, equivalent to 1.2 million kettles being turned on at once, if England made it into the later stages of the 2010 FIFA World Cup. The system operator must be able to balance supply and demand, which it does by buying ancillary services in a real-time market.

All of the above can be achieved by relying solely on the market functioning. In fact, the shift from top-down regulatory choices to a decentralised process based on demand and supply interactions shaped the energy revolution that has occurred in the EU – starting in the UK – over the past 30 years. Markets for electricity can and do work, as long as they are not jeopardised by other policies.

PART 2

LIBERALISATION IN ADVANCE AND RETREAT

It seems to me that this is theoretically right, for whatever the question under discussion – whether religious, philosophical, political, or economic; whether it concerns prosperity, morality, equality, right, justice, progress, responsibility, cooperation, property, labor, trade, capital, wages, taxes, population, finance, or government – at whatever point on the scientific horizon I begin my researches, I invariably reach this one conclusion: The solution to the problems of human relationships is to be found in liberty.

Frédéric Bastiat (1998: 73)

6 THE EU BEFORE THE 'LIBERALISATION' OF ELECTRICITY

The rise of the European regulatory state

In the late 1980s, a vertically integrated, state-owned monopoly was the normal way of providing electricity throughout Europe. With the exception of Great Britain and Norway (which is not an EU member state) (Jamasb and Pollitt 2005; Amundsen et al. 2006), there was also little debate about who should be in charge of running the power system, making forecasts of future demand, setting prices and planning investments. The idea of a 'market' for electricity was deeply unfashionable.

At the same time, the European unification process included an important energy component. Since the inception of the EU, energy was a major part of the international treaties that laid the foundations of what was then known as the European Economic Community. The first proposal for integration came from the French Foreign Minister Robert Schuman (1950), who, on 9 May 1950, suggested establishing a supranational community with the aim of '[making] war not only unthinkable but materially impossible'. From an economic standpoint, something can be made impossible by making it too costly. The most obvious way to make war between nations too costly is to increase the commercial ties between them. The six member countries created the European Coal and Steel Community (ECSC), which was formally established with the Treaty of Paris in 1951. The Treaty laid the conditions for a common market for coal and steel.

A few years later, the Euratom Treaty and the Treaty of Rome itself were signed on 25 March 1957. The former followed in the ECSC's footsteps by covering nuclear power, which was then seen as the energy source that would meet virtually all of humanity's needs in the future.[1] The latter established the European Economic Community, an organisation that was specifically devoted to developing the institutions of a common market in order to achieve a deeper integration. A political goal – peace – was to be pursued trough economic means: economic integration and free trade (Harris 2001). A few years later, in 1965, the three communities would be subsumed under the Merger Treaty, also called the Brussels Treaty, and the modern history of the European Community began. The EU was intended to be about integrating markets no less than about creating political superstructures and a new bureaucracy.

In a way, both energy and market integration are at the heart of the EU. However, a truly integrated market for energy has not yet been developed. There are good reasons for this. Firstly, no country among the original six – let alone those that would join over time – even had a domestic market for energy (particularly electricity). All of them relied on state monopolies. Secondly, energy was regarded as a highly sensitive national security matter. Nation states (rather than Europe as a whole) tried to become as energy-independent as possible (France would pursue this policy in the most extreme way, forging an electricity system that was

---

1   The common wisdom about nuclear power since the end of World War II is well captured by a famous quote from Lewis Strauss, chairman of the US Atomic Energy Commission, who said: 'Our children will enjoy in their homes electrical energy too cheap to meter ... It is not too much to expect that our children will know of great periodic regional famines in the world only as matters of history, will travel effortlessly over the seas and under them and through the air with a minimum of danger and at great speeds, and will experience a lifespan far longer than ours, as disease yields and man comes to understand what causes him to age'. It should be underlined, though, that Strauss had in mind the developments of fusion, not fission, technologies. See Pfau (1985).

largely supplied by domestic nuclear power). Furthermore, there was an obvious link between the civilian use of nuclear power and its potential military use.[2] The absence of markets in energy was also justified by the fact that the natural monopoly issue was regarded as insurmountable. In addition, the intellectual climate at the time was inherently hostile to the idea of deregulating energy. How did Europe move from widespread state monopolies to liberalisation and privatisation? It relied on four drivers:

* budget constraints meant that the shortcomings of the public monopolies became evident;
* technological developments created favourable conditions for liberalisation;
* the intellectual and political pendulum was swinging towards a belief in a free economy pushed by the end of the Cold War and Britain's success story;
* the interest of the EU's own bureaucracies.

The European Commission's role in 'promoting' a 'free market' in energy

It would be naïve to believe that the EU bureaucracy has a philosophical commitment to a free market. It does, of course, like any other bureaucracy, have a strong incentive to maximise its own power and influence. But, as far as energy is concerned, the treaties did not leave much room for direct intervention from Brussels. Moreover, the EU budget could not be invested in energy projects with some relatively modest exceptions for research and development and for 'strategic' infrastructures. As paradoxical as it may seem, the UK's experiment with electricity deregulation provided a new perspective. In Britain, electricity restructuring

---

2 On the fallacies of energy independence, see Bryce (2009); on energy security as a good that can be efficiently priced by the market, see Robinson (2006).

led to a major change in the role of the state from provider to regulator (on the British case, see the next chapter). After all, some regulation was still deemed necessary, at least for the natural monopoly aspect of electricity provision.

Although no new powers were given to the European Commission and the EU Parliament until 2009,[3] they did have powers to regulate competition and the environment. Thus, the British model, if copied, could provide a regulatory route into energy markets for the Commission. As Moran (2003: 17) explains:

> At the level of the EU, conversely, the rise of regulation is due to the very lack of modes of command. The Union has neither the budget-raising capacity nor the bureaucratic muscle to impose policies on either national members or sectional interests. Promulgating regulations potentially solves this problem.

The power-maximising attitude of any bureaucracy explains much of what has been done in the energy sector at the EU level. This includes outcomes that have raised costs (such as climate policies) and outcomes that have promoted efficiency, such as the liberalisation of energy markets outside Britain.

There is, though, a major difference between the EU and the UK experience. In Britain, liberalisations would have been unthinkable without the political willpower of Margaret Thatcher, her ministers and leading academic and other intellectual figures. Of course, powerful vested interests were contesting the liberalisation process, but the political leadership had a clear vision.

At the EU level, things were very different. Firstly, there was no open political push behind energy liberalisations. Market

---

3   This remained true until 2009, when the Treaty of Lisbon came into effect. Article 194(1) of the Treaty of Lisbon defines the new powers of the Commission with regard to energy policy in reference to (a) ensuring the functioning of the energy market, (b) ensuring security of supply, (c) promoting sustainability and (d) promoting interconnections of energy networks. See Braun (2011).

opening was never seen as a political shift that was grounded on a different view of how the economy should work. It was, rather, a technocratic option to achieve a more efficient management of the power system (as well as a tool to increase Brussels's regulatory powers). Secondly, it was not just private vested interests that were involved: national governments had their own vested interests, and they acted accordingly. Most EU member states had state-owned incumbents. Accepting competition inside their borders would have weakened those incumbents, reduced the government's ability to interfere with the economy and, in some countries, reduced a range of patronage opportunities.

Nevertheless, it was in this climate that some liberalisation measures took place. Three waves of directives were passed after very long debates on what should be included and what latitude could be granted to national governments in implementing the directives (see Chapter 8). The three liberalisation packages came together with a number of other regulations that had to do with the promotion of renewable energy, emissions reductions, security of supply, research and development, etc. Figure 4 shows the timetable for the EU regulatory framework's development. We will only deal with electricity liberalisation and the promotion of green energy sources, but the reader should always remember that these measures came together with many others, and that the interaction of different measures can cause perverse effects (Abrell and Weigt 2008; Braathen 2011).

The intellectual and political foundation of the EU path towards liberalisation may be defined with regard to three main topics (Serrales 2006): third-party access (TPA), consumer choice and network unbundling.

Third-party access has to do with the non-discriminatory management of, and open access to, essential facilities (those parts of the system that are possibly natural monopolies). Consumer choice involves the ability of consumers to freely choose their supplier, and it presupposes the existence of an unregulated

Figure 4 EU legislative framework for energy

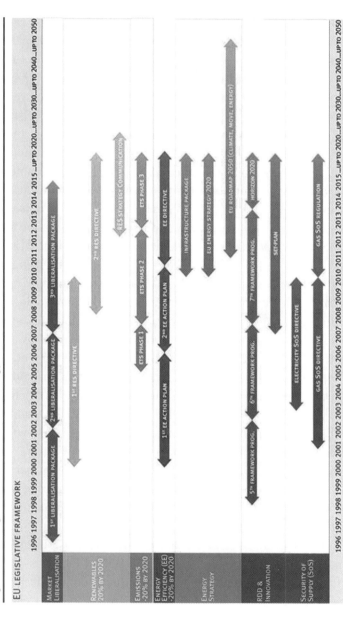

Source: Eurelectric.

40

price system. To achieve this, the interests of the incumbent need to be separated from those of the system operator. The first EU liberalisation package focused on TPA; the second wave dealt with consumer choice, and the third was about network unbundling. Before the content of the relevant EU directives is described, we will discuss in more detail the British experience. What happened in the UK between the late 1980s and mid-1990s is of huge importance. It provided much of the institutional experimentation that helped to show the rest of Europe that there are alternative ways to a state monopoly to organise electricity systems. The British model also proved to be more successful than the state monopoly in several respects.

It is worth noting that, after the initial period of exciting institutional experimentation in Britain, there was a slow down and then a reversal, with the market tending back towards more state control. The EU also adopted a number of measures that, while having little direct impact on competition, significantly changed the way operators behave. In both cases, at the heart of the regulatory attack that has reversed the process of liberalisation there was a misguided idea of how to deal with the problem of climate change.

7 LIBERALISING ELECTRICITY MARKETS THE BRITISH WAY

It would be impossible to understand the switch from vertically integrated, state-owned monopolies to liberalised markets without taking into consideration a major political shift that took place in the 1980s. That shift had a substantial effect on how several industries were regulated as well as on the role of the state in the economy in a broader sense. The place where the pendulum swung the furthest was Great Britain.

The main character behind this change was, of course, Prime Minister Thatcher. When Margaret Thatcher assumed office, she may not have had a clear vision of how to deal with energy policy. She wanted to address energy security after the oil shocks, and she also wanted to reduce the power of unions, especially in the coal industry. Moreover, a general distrust of state-owned companies led to an investigation of important state-owned energy businesses, which, in turn, led to a conclusion that, in retrospect, was not surprising at all. The formal investigation from the Monopolies and Mergers Commission showed (Helm 2003: 51):

excess output, keeping [coal] pits open and building too many stations; financial laxity in planning and project execution; prices set at artificially low levels relative to costs; and labour bias and overstaffing. Add these to the familiar problem of shorter-term political interference (usually done in private, rather than in terms of any direction through published guidance) and it is remarkable that their Morrisonian structure had lasted so long. By the early 1980s, the nationalised industries had built up sufficient inefficiencies to warrant more radical surgery.

Even this would not have been enough to precipitate major reform in the absence of a clear political will. The paradigm shift happened under Lord (Nigel) Lawson, who was Secretary of State for Energy from 1981–83 (and later Chancellor of the Exchequer from 1983–89). He anticipated the change in a seminal speech (Lawson 1982) that laid down the foundations of a major shift in the way energy policy in general, and within the electricity industry in particular, had to be pursued:

> I do not see the government's task as being to try to plan the future shape of energy production and consumption. It is not even primarily to try to balance UK demand and supply for energy. Our task is rather to set a framework which will ensure that the market operates in the energy sector with a minimum of distortion and that energy is produced and consumed efficiently.

> ... The government's role is neither to induce the individual to take decisions against his better judgement, nor to waste public money in subsidising investment that is already worthwhile. The way to bring the two sides together and to ensure that they act consistently is to give them the same information and the same realistic signals.

> ... Most of the supply industries in the UK are state-owned. In part, state-ownership came about as a means of regulating natural monopoly. But this has not always been the case; and it is time to question both the extent of the natural monopoly and, when it can be shown to exist, the most effective means of regulation. State-ownership is neither a vital necessity nor the only means of regulation.

This set in motion a long process that would lead to the liberalisation of the electricity market and the privatisation of former monopolies. The view about how to proceed was clear from the beginning, as emerges from the so-called Littlechild Report of 1983. This set the stage for the price-cap regulation formula under which all the British utilities were privatised (see Littlechild 1983; Bartle 2003).

Britain provided a case study for the combination of liberalisation and privatisation that might be successfully employed to achieve a restructuring of the power sector. The process helped to increase the economic efficiency of energy production and consumption, reduce the burden on taxpayers and power consumers, set appropriate incentives and create the conditions for technological improvements and innovation.

It is no surprise that the EU, though in a very cautious way and while mediating between different interests and intellectual or political pressures from member states, followed the British model of restructuring to some extent.

The core of the British model

The British model of liberalisation relied on three pillars: ownership unbundling and price-cap regulation of the natural monopoly, deregulated wholesale and retail markets, and privatisation. One reason why the EU-led liberalisation fell short of expectations is that Brussels immediately gave up privatisation (Stagnaro 2014a) and has traditionally been weak in requesting member states to implement meaningful liberalisation at the retail level (Benedettini and Stagnaro 2015). Interestingly enough, the most recent documents on the so-called Energy Union place more emphasis on this latter point (EC 2015a,b).

Ownership unbundling is a direct consequence of a better understanding of how the industry works. It was made possible also by technological developments that reduced the costs of coordination between those operating at different stages of the industry. An important step forward was the acknowledgment that, while networks tend to show some characteristics of a natural monopoly, other activities within the industry – such as generation, retail and marketing – can gain from a competitive environment. This led to the separation of such activities.

In this way, two goals were met simultaneously. Competition was made possible, and the need for regulation was then reduced as a consequence. While there is still a lot of discussion about the costs and benefits of vertical separation, the British experience (as well as that of a few other countries) provides evidence that the benefits outweigh the costs (Pollitt 2008a). The successful separation of networks from the former monopolists, as well as the provision that no market agent can own transmission and distribution networks, is a key component of the British model. It made it possible for the market to develop as well as for newcomers to confidently enter this market.

Ownership unbundling would have little effect if it were not complemented by wholesale and retail market deregulation – that is, by free entry and the ability of consumers to switch suppliers. The very raison d'être of ownership unbundling lies in making competition possible both at the generation and wholesale level and at the retail level.

There is much discussion among economists and policymakers about the effectiveness of retail competition, even though a growing amount of evidence suggests that it can deliver relevant benefits both price-wise and by promoting innovation (Kiesling 2015). There is more agreement on the desirable consequences of a competitive environment at the generation and wholesale market levels. However, it is harder than one might believe to draw a line between wholesale and retail markets. One lesson from the British experience in the 1990s and early 2000s is precisely that a reform is more successful if it is conceived as a consistent set of measures aimed at changing the functioning of an entire industry. Keeping elements of liberalisation together with elements of state control, as many EU member states did, undermines the credibility of reform.

The liberalisation of retail and wholesale markets resulted in the expected consequences. There was lively competition; it created a plurality of commercial offers aimed at meeting the consumers' different needs; product differentiation was promoted (which is quite remarkable, given that electricity has been traditionally treated as an undifferentiated commodity); and there was downward pressure on prices. Every statistic about prices, industry concentration and consumer switching between suppliers tells a story of success (Acer 2014). From 1990 to 1999, electricity charges for domestic consumers fell by 26 per cent in real terms (Littlechild 2000), with a larger fall for industrial users. It cannot be argued that this was only due to a fall in world energy prices. The whole point is that, until privatisation, electricity companies had to use expensive domestic fuels and were not subject to pressure towards greater efficiency.

The initial success of the British experience relied on taking regulatory powers away from the government and giving them to an independent regulatory body. The architects of liberalisation believed that the price control powers of the regulator (now called Ofgem, but originally called OFFER) should be a temporary tool that was necessary to enable the transition from the state-owned, vertically integrated monopoly to free-market competition within a vertically unbundled industry.

The third pillar of the British experience, which has never really entered into European policy, was privatisation. Part of the motivation for privatisation was that it was believed that, despite all the measures that were put in place to avoid regulatory capture, a state-owned utility was much more likely to be successful in capturing the regulator than a private one. If a state-owned utility were to be favoured by the regulator, effective competition would be much more difficult to achieve. Even if actual competition were not constrained by state ownership, potential competition is limited, because new entrants would fear that they would not be treated fairly (Beesley and Littlechild 1983, 1989; Myddelton 2014).

The central role of privatisation is a unique feature of the British experience with liberalisation, and perhaps it is the feature that allowed the UK to get as far as it did, not least because it was effective in promoting competition.

The British retreat from the British model

Re-regulation of the UK electricity market

In recent years, a number of policy changes have happened in Britain, such that it can now hardly be described as a model for electricity liberalisation (even though it is still the most liberalised country in Europe – see Benedettini 2014a, 2015). Every feature of the British model has come under attack, and it has been or is being 'reformed' in a way that consistently drives the decision-making process towards greater centralisation and politicisation. Regulation was originally conceived as a necessary bridge towards a progressively deregulated environment. However, regulation increasingly aims at higher political goals, justified on the grounds of following industrial, environmental, energy security and consumer protection policies. The strongest alibi for this movement towards re-regulation was provided by climate change.

Regulation is now used in the UK to pursue politically driven targets rather than to ensure that markets serve consumers. This involves a considerable degree of discretionary power. Even if there are goals that the consumers may wish to see achieved but that the market may not in general deliver (such as a reduction in carbon emissions), these can be achieved by relying on technology-neutral policies, which have little or no impact on the competitive dynamics of the market. Unfortunately, British policymakers – in common with those in other parts of the EU – have pursued policies that promote the goal of reducing carbon emissions in ways that are inconsistent with the principles of a free market. The functioning of the market has therefore been undermined. In response, there has been a vicious circle of intervention to address distortions, followed by further interventions. There remains policy incoherence in the market design, and conflicting targets are being assigned to market operators.

Liberalisation is under attack from several fronts. The most important ones are the price-formation mechanism and the requirement of the market to deliver investments in clean technologies.

Price controls and interference in industrial structure

As far as prices are concerned, in 2015 the Labour Party proposed a price freeze as well as an obligation for companies to ring-fence their generation businesses from their supply businesses (Flint 2014), though they were not elected. The newly elected Labour leader, Jeremy Corbyn, has gone as far as to propose the renationalisation of the energy industry (Pickard 2015). In fact, prices are already subject to severe regulations. Ofgem, the UK's energy regulator, has imposed obligations regarding the nature and number of offers and tariffs that suppliers can make to consumers, as well as in relation to the underlying pricing policy (Littlechild 2014). These regulatory interventions have reduced the market's ability to satisfy consumers' needs, prevented certain forms of price undercutting by energy firms and stopped them developing special niche, good-value tariffs. Ofgem (and, potentially, the government) is making choices on behalf of consumers because, in effect, it is believed that consumers are unable to discern the best-value tariff. Ironically, the British Competition and Markets Authority (CMA) has recently issued a report on the electricity market, which showed how such regulations harm rather than benefit consumers (CMA 2015a).

The proposal to separate generation and supply businesses – which has a lot of support - is also inconsistent with a liberalised framework. While a strong case can be made for unbundling network operation (the natural monopoly) from generation and supply (the competitive part of the market), within the rest of the system there is no optimal degree of integration that can be predetermined by government. Competition – as can be inferred from price dynamics and switching rates (Benedettini and Stagnaro 2015) – is the result of choices by consumers and businesses, including a choice between firms that have different forms of industrial organisation.[1] If firms are prevented from differentiating themselves from each other, the market will be denied the opportunity to discover the most efficient form of corporate organisation. Ultimately, companies will ask the same price for an undifferentiated service, and the consumer will have no interest in switching. The process of competition involves allowing firms to do things differently, as each firm strives for efficiency. The above-mentioned CMA report found that vertical integration was not, in fact, a problem in the market.[2]

Electricity market reform – back to central planning

Liberalisation is not only under pressure on the retail side. A more fundamental attack came with the approval of UK Electricity

---

1   On the theory of industrial organisation, see Coase (1937) and Williamson (1975, 1985).

2   The same report argues that consumer inertia is a problem insofar as it allows suppliers to exercise market power. In order to protect disengaged consumers, the CMA proposes the introduction of a 'transitional safeguard regulated tariff' (CMA 2015b) for those consumers who do not catch the opportunities from switching supplier. It goes beyond the scope of this monograph to deal with such a complex issue. A critical discussion of the CMA proposal can be found in Littlechild et al. (2015) and Stagnaro and Booth (2015).

Market Reform (ERM) (DECC 2012; Verde 2012; Allen and Overy 2012). This dramatically changes the drivers of investment decisions. Not surprisingly, the official aim of the reform is the protection of the environment, with particular reference to climate policy. The government's commitment to promote the economy's decarbonisation through top-down regulations and a fundamental revision of electricity market design, which was begun under the previous coalition government, is unlikely to change after the Conservative victory in May 2015 (Tindale 2015), despite a growing concern for the potential cost of renewable incentives. According to the Department of Energy and Climate Change (DECC), the core of the Reform lies in the following provisions:[3]

- Contracts for difference (CFD), which are long-term contracts that provide stable and predictable incentives for companies to invest in low-carbon generation.

- A capacity market to ensure the security of electricity supply, including provisions to allow electricity demand reduction to be delivered.

- Conflicts of interest and contingency arrangements to ensure the institution that will deliver these schemes is fit for purpose.

- Investment contracts, which are long-term contracts that enabled early investment in advance of the CFD regime that came into force in 2014.

- Access to markets, which includes 'power purchase agreements' (PPAs), to ensure the availability of long-term contracts for independent renewable generators, and liquidity measures to enable the government to take action to improve the liquidity of the electricity market, should it prove necessary.

---

3   See www.gov.uk/government/collections/energy-act. For a broader description, see also the EMR webpage: https://www.gov.uk/government/publications/2010-to-2015-government-policy-uk-energy-security/2010-to-2015-government-policy-uk-energy-security#appendix-5-electricity-market-reform-emr

- Renewables transitional arrangements for investments under the 'renewables obligation scheme'.

- An emissions performance standard (EPS) to limit CO_2 emissions from new fossil fuel power stations.

A broader discussion of EMR can be found in Robinson (2013), who summarised its effects as follows: 'government is once more deeply involved in major energy investment decisions about which it lacks relevant knowledge'. Beyond the effect in relation to each specific provision, what matters is that the reform changes the landscape in two ways. On the one hand the government – not market operators – will effectively make technological decisions by setting up discretionary subsidies and/or mandates for different technologies. In doing so, the British government is effectively socialising at least some portion of the investment risk and artificially changing the prices and risks involved in investing in different technologies. Ultimately, the government is setting the long-term composition of UK energy generating capacity just as it did from the 1970s to the 1980s, when the government encouraged coal and nuclear energy generation. The government is also changing the operators' incentives, as well as their very way of doing business, by remunerating the capacity they provide in addition to the energy they sell (see also Chapter 16).

A good example of the underlying risks can be found in the decision to subsidise a new nuclear plant at Hinkley Point C (Beckman 2014; van Renssen 2014a). A strike price[4] has been awarded for a 30-year period, effectively guaranteeing that electricity can be sold by the investors at a price about twice the current wholesale price of electricity in the UK. The new investment will not just displace investments in other technologies, it will crowd out non-subsidised investments in which the taxpayer does not

---

4   The strike price has been set at 92.50 £/MWh. A strike price acts as a fixed price for nuclear energy: if wholesale prices are above the strike price, the utility will return the difference to the consumers; if, instead, they fall below it, the generator will receive a top-up payment.

bear the risk. Ironically, the new cycle of British energy policy intervention begins where the old one left off – subsidising large, costly nuclear plants (Henderson 2013).

Paradoxically, such decisions come after (and despite) the failure of earlier renewable policies in the UK (Gross 2010), the rethinking of renewable policies in several EU member states (including Germany, Spain and Italy, which used to be the most enthusiastic supporters of green subsidies)[5] and after a significant recalibration of EU climate policy with regard to the 2030 targets (Glachant 2014).

The U-turn on electricity liberalisation in the UK is likely to have consequences not just for Britain but for the whole of the EU. Ironically, the liberalisation framework that was set up in the 1990s did not fail in delivering to consumers what they sought; neither did it fail in allowing producers to take risks or make profits. In fact, the liberalisation failed to make consumers and producers make the choices that policymakers believed were best for them. In other words, the UK's electricity liberalisation failed to work like a centralised, state-run system: it failed politically because it succeeded economically.

---

5   On Germany, see *The Economist* (2014); on Spain, see *The Economist* (2013); on Italy, see Stagnaro (2014b).

PART 3

THE EU, ELECTRICITY DEREGULATION AND CLIMATE-DRIVEN REGULATION

Two main alternative views of the regulation of industry are widely held. The first is that regulation is instituted primarily for the protection and benefit of the public at large or some large subclass of the public. In this view, the regulations which injure the public – as when the oil import quotas increase the cost of petroleum products to America by $5 billion or more a year – are costs of some social goal (here, national defense) or, occasionally, perversions of the regulatory philosophy. The second view is essentially that the political process defies rational explanation: 'politics' is an imponderable, a constantly and unpredictably shifting mixture of forces of the most diverse nature, comprehending acts of great moral virtue (the emancipation of slaves) and of the most vulgar venality (the congressman feathering his own nest).

George J. Stigler (1971: 3)

8 LIBERALISING ELECTRICITY MARKETS THE EU WAY

The first liberalisation package

The EU implemented three packages of directives and regulations aimed at progressively opening national electricity markets and promoting their integration (see Figure 4 on page 40). These packages have been relatively successful in meeting their stated objectives, but they have not created a full paradigm shift. The reversal of the trend towards liberalisation in Britain makes it more unlikely than ever that policy will change in the EU.

The first package of liberalisation directives was passed in 1996 (Directive 1996/92/EC), with an obligation for the member states to translate it into national legislation by 1998. The aim of the Directive was to create the basic conditions for competition to develop, rather than to introduce competition directly.

The Directive introduced three concepts that were revolutionary at the time, although they proved insufficient. Vertical integration was challenged by introducing a requirement for functional unbundling, whereby the essential facilities operator was to be managed in a transparent way and targeted by ad hoc regulations, although it could still be controlled by the vertically integrated monopolist. In addition, access to the essential facilities was required to be free for all competitors on a non-discriminatory basis. Finally, generators were supposed to be free to compete with each other, and newcomers were allowed to invest in new generation capacity.

The Commission itself (EC 2007a: §331) describes the aims of the Directive as follows:

The Directive removed legal monopolies by requiring Member States gradually to allow large electricity customers to choose their suppliers (concept of 'eligibility'). It also obliged vertically integrated companies to grant third parties access to their transmission and distribution networks ('third party access'). Furthermore, for vertically integrated companies active in generation, transmission and supply it finally mandated a minimum level of separation of the network business from the other activities ('unbundling'). In a nutshell the Directive introduced the distinction between a regulated part of the market (network) and competitive parts of the market (generation and supply).

The Directive did not achieve the expected results. This was probably due to the latitude allowed to member states in implementing its provisions. For example, by allowing accounting separation rather than requiring the incorporation of system operators as fully-fledged companies, the Directive left much space for opportunistic behaviours. Moreover, most incumbents were still state owned, and there was no pressure towards privatisation. Finally, regulatory functions were left to governments that had too much of a conflict of interest, given that they owned and controlled the incumbent companies.

However, some good did come from the Directive. It affirmed an important principle that gradually came to be accepted: namely that, in the long run, vertically integrated monopolies should be broken up, and regulation should be pursued by independent regulatory bodies.

The second liberalisation package

Over time, a consensus emerged that the partial failure of the first liberalisation package stemmed from the ambiguities embodied in the Directive's language. While the EU markets had been formally opened, it was the former monopolies that were still dominant.

It is under these conditions that the second liberalisation package was devised. This time, the impulse was stronger. The second Directive (2003/54/EC) was adopted in 2003 and was to be transposed in national legislation by 2004. This package focused on fixing the most ineffective provisions of the first Directive, implementing clearer rules with regard to essential facilities and unbundling, ensuring the pursuit of regulation by independent bodies and opening up competition at the retail level for any group of consumers.

EC (2007a: §§ 333–39) summarises the intentions of the Directive as follows:

The Second Electricity Directive aimed at complete market opening. It required that all non-household electricity customers became eligible by 1 July 2004. This will be followed by the opening of the electricity markets for all household customers by 1 July 2007. This approach will remove the discrepancies in the level of market opening between Member States.

The Second Electricity Directive obliges Member States to introduce a "regulated third party access" regime under which third parties have a right to access the network in a non-discriminatory manner based on published tariffs. The Directive removes the possibility of negotiated third party access regimes, which were considered not to sufficiently mitigate the market power of networks owners, vis à vis the alternative of regulated third party access regimes.

In order to ensure efficient and constant supervision of fair network access, the Second Electricity Directive mandates the appointment of a national regulator that is independent from the electricity industry (but not necessarily independent from governments). The regulators must monitor the overall activities of the network companies, deal with complaints, and control network tariffs, a key element in creating competitive conditions.

In order to limit further the risks of discrimination and cross subsidies associated with the existence of vertically integrated companies the Directive requires legal unbundling – in addition to accounting and management unbundling – between network activities (transmission and distribution) and all other activities. In practice this means that transmission and distribution System Operators must be independent in their legal form, organisation and decision making. However a holding company is still entitled to approve the annual financial plan and to set global limits on the level of indebtedness.

The Directive permits the postponement of legal unbundling of distribution companies until 1 July 2007 and allows Member States to exempt them from the legal unbundling obligation altogether if the distribution companies serve less than 100,000 connected customers.

Despite the usual resistance from national governments and state-owned incumbents, the outcome was more encouraging than that of the first package. By 2007, all EU member states had implemented regulated – rather than negotiated – TPA to networks; most of them had set up transparent wholesale markets, created the conditions for every consumer to be free to choose their supplier and moved from vertical integration to legal unbundling (though ownership unbundling was adopted in a few countries).

Yet, reforms in many countries again fell short of expectations, particularly with regard to the separation of transmission and distribution networks from vertically integrated monopolies. Many member states left the networks in the hands of incumbents, merely trying to mitigate the potential anti-competitive outcomes through regulation. This led to a great deal of regulation and, in some cases, a very opaque background for the industry. For this reason, the Commission proceeded to the third liberalisation package.

The third liberalisation package

The main problems with the first and second liberalisation packages were the ambiguous treatment of networks and the insufficient pressure on retail liberalisation. The third liberalisation package tried to address the former issue. However, the resistance from national governments and former monopolists was so strong that Brussels fell short one more time. Directive 2009/72/ CE was largely a compromise between the theoretical goal of eventually breaking up monopolies and the inconvenient truth of the powerful lobbying of those monopolies.

Some results were, in fact, achieved. Ownership unbundling is clearly defined in Article 1(11) of the Directive as 'the most effective tool by which to promote investments in infrastructure in a non-discriminatory way, fair access to the network for new entrants and transparency in the market'. Unfortunately, despite the clear preference for ownership unbundling, a loophole was left to member states, allowing them to set up an independent system operator (ISO) or an independent transmission operator (ITO) as an alternative to ownership unbundling (OU). Both ISOs and ITOs require a very burdensome regulatory apparatus, in order to make sure that the essential facility, although owned or controlled by a vertically integrated company, acts as a truly independent entity.

When it came to retail liberalisation, the implementation was even more loose. However, despite its limits, even the third liberalisation package was useful for promoting market opening across Europe as well as for creating the conditions to have more energy trading between member states. The need to pursue greater market integration, with specific regard to retail markets, has made a comeback in the most recent European Commission communications on the so-called Energy Union (EC 2015a,b). The average market share of incumbent dominant firms in the EU fell from 64.9 per cent in 1999 to 55.9 per cent in 2010. In the meantime, several private and foreign companies entered markets that, until then, had been treated as inherently monopolistic and had been left in the hands of state-owned companies. Table 1 summarises the progress and the political choices underlying the liberalisation process.

Overall, the results of reform were not trivial. Indirect evidence of increasing market integration comes from the gradual market coupling that is happening as cross-border trade (and physical power flows) grow and prices tend to converge between different markets (EC 2012). Whilst, in the past, member states had tended to not properly implement the electricity directives, which led to the opening of infringement procedures, such procedures are being progressively closed, a sign that EU markets are in the process of gradually being opened to competition. ERGEG (2010) recognises that there have been 'some positive developments, especially on wholesale markets and at power exchanges', even though many more opportunities remain to be captured. The functioning of wholesale markets is progressively being harmonised in order to increase the market's physical as well as financial scope.

The progress made so far is reflected in the Organisation for Economic Co-operation and Development (OECD) Product Market Regulation report. This measures the intensity of competition in a number of markets, including electricity (Conway and Nicoletti 2006; Koske et al. 2015). The report includes several indicators, most of which are of a qualitative nature. It examines how the market is designed, and how decisions are made. It does not look at the outcomes in terms of pricing and the number of competitors (although concentration indexes may be used in relevant

Table 1 Achievements of EU electricity directives

	Most common form pre-1996	*1996 Directive*	*2003 Directive*	*2009 Directive*
Generation	Monopoly	Authorisation tendering	Authorisation	Authorisation
Transmission and distribution	Monopoly	Regulated TPA Negotiated TPA Single buyer	Regulated TPA	Regulated TPA
Supply	Monopoly	Accounting separation	Legal separation from transmission and distribution	Ownership separation from transmission and distribution Legal separation from transmission and distribution under ISO/ITO arrangements
Customers	No choice	Choice for eligible customers	All non-household consumers have choice (2004) All consumers have choice (2007)	All consumers have choice
Unbundling of transmission and distribution	None	Accounts	Legal	Ownership Legal under ISO/ITO
Cross-border trade	Monopoly	Negotiated	Regulated	Regulated
Regulation	Government department	Not specified	Independent regulatory body	Independent regulatory body

Source: Vasconcelos (2004) with author's additions.

discussion in the document and/or as a proxy for the existence of legal barriers to competition). In most European countries, the degree of competition increased steadily over time, as is shown by Figure 5 (where lower scores are associated with more competitive environments).

Figure 5 Regulatory conditions in the electricity sector (1975–2013) in Europe

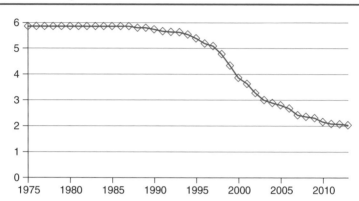

Source: adaptation of OECD data. Note: a complete series is available for 21 of the EU member states; the EU-wide indicator has been estimated as the unweighted average of these 21 countries.

Under the Product Market Regulation methodology, a market scores better if entry is unrestricted, there is no state ownership, market concentration indices are low enough and switching rates are high enough to prevent any supplier (or consumer) from exercising market power. Of course, the steps in the right direction that have been taken are not just due to the EU market opening, and the fact that the UK started to open up its market in the 1980s certainly cannot be credited to the EU; but the kind of progress that can be observed would have been unthinkable without EU pressure upon most national governments in Europe.

These steps did not come without a cost. To achieve liberalisation, there has been a degree of harmonisation that is probably higher than necessary, together with a shift of regulatory powers from the national level to the EU and a subsequent over-regulation of many areas. Although this shift of powers was needed to some extent, it reduces the scope for institutional evolution and experimentation. It has also resulted in too much regulation with regard to consumer protection and the industrial models of network development.

However, the more serious issue, where regulation has been more aggressive and distortionary, is in the area of environmental regulation, especially with regard to climate-related regulations and the promotion of renewable energy. While the liberalisation effort has resulted in more decentralisation and less government control, the promotion of renewable energies through subsidies and mandates has pushed in the opposite direction.

9 ENVIRONMENTAL REGULATION: THE EMPIRE STRIKES BACK

Renewable energy: environmental policy or industrial policy?

The EU made a distinctive mark in its willingness to decarbonise its economy unilaterally, pursuing the Kyoto Protocol goals (Kyoto being the international treaty signed back in 1997 that was designed to unite all industrialised economies in a common effort to cut emissions jointly to 5.2 per cent below 1990 levels by 2012). After several moves back and forth, a comprehensive set of climate policies was adopted by the EU. In particular, there was the so-called 20-20-20 package (EC 2007b). This package sets three targets to be reached by 2020: cutting emissions by 20 per cent below 1990 levels, increasing the share of renewable energy up to 20 per cent of total consumption and increasing energy efficiency by 20 per cent. This latter goal was non-binding and will not be discussed in detail.

To achieve the target, a cap-and-trade scheme called the Emissions Trading Scheme (ETS) was created, which became operational in 2005. The market price of allowances reflected the marginal cost of CO_2 abatement: in theory, if transaction costs are low enough, the system will allow those who have high marginal abatement costs to buy allowances from those who have low marginal abatement costs, and emissions cuts will be made where it is cheaper. The ETS as designed has many shortcomings, but they are not relevant at this stage of the argument.

The other pillar of EU environmental policy (or energy policy) is the promotion of renewable energy sources. Pro-renewables policies started in the 1990s, but it was only after the 20-20-20 package that they became the core of a broad policy that ranges from the promotion of biofuels to renewable sources of electrical supply. Electricity is particularly prone to renewable penetration, because technologies already exist – albeit often inefficient ones only made viable through generous subsidies – that may, in principle, be easily integrated into the power system. The Commission intervened directly on renewables with two directives. The following sections will examine those directives.

The first renewable energy sources directive

The first Directive on Electricity Production from Renewable Energy Sources (2001/77/EC) set national targets for EU member states that aimed at reaching a 21 per cent target for electricity generated from green sources. According to the EU's Summary of Legislation:

> The Member States must adopt and publish, initially every five years, a report setting the indicative Member State targets for future RES-E [Renewable Energy Sources for Electricity] consumption for the following ten years and showing what measures have or are to be taken to meet those targets. The Member State targets must take account of the reference values set out in the Annex to the Directive for Member States' indicative targets concerning the share of electricity produced from renewable energy sources in gross electricity consumption in 2010. They must also be compatible with all the national commitments entered into as part of the commitments accepted by the Community in Kyoto.[1]

---

1 http://europa.eu/legislation_summaries/energy/renewable_energy/ l27035_en.htm.

Member states were left free to choose the policy tools they deemed the most appropriate to meet the goal, provided that they were consistent with more general EU regulations regarding the internal market for energy and the principle of freedom of movement and establishment for EU companies. National governments were, in fact, supposed to adopt different schemes that levelled the playing field for different renewables over time. In truth, at the time the Directive came into force, most green energies were so far from being competitive that they were awarded significant subsidies and incentives.

Three major tools emerged for promoting renewables.

- Capital subsidies (or tax breaks) to install renewable capacity.

- Green certificate schemes, under which, for every unit of green energy, a green certificate is released. Power producers are assigned a minimum amount of green energy that corresponds to a given number of green certificates they have to surrender by the end of the year. In order to do so, they can either produce green energy by themselves or buy certificates from others. As in the case of cap-and-trade, the theory suggests that green energy will actually be produced by the most efficient generators.

- Feed-in tariffs or feed-in premiums, whereby a given source of energy – say, solar power – is awarded a monetary incentive for every kWh that is produced.[2]

Generally speaking, these subsidy schemes were accompanied by another crucial provision: member states have to grant

---

2 Feed-in tariffs are long-term contracts with an investor, who is granted a given price for the energy it produces for a given period of time. Feed-in premiums differ from feed-in tariffs insofar as they do not set a purchase price but rather a premium that the generator obtains on top of the market price for energy. The difference between the two schemes, therefore, is that the investor who subscribes to a feed-in tariff is not exposed to variations in the value of energy as a commodity, while the investor who subscribes to a feed-in premium is. See Couture (2010).

either priority access or guaranteed access to the grid for 'green' electricity.

In this way, green energy was liberated from any risk on the demand side: whatever the amount of green energy to be generated, it would be dispatched to the end user, and the remuneration for green energy would be set by regulatory fiat. In the years following the adoption of the directive, large subsidies were paid for renewables. Given the cost, however, renewable energy still remained marginal despite the subsidy, though growth in output was rapid. The most cost-effective sources (such as hydropower), which had traditionally played a significant role in some energy markets, did not grow much for other reasons.[3]

The efforts to promote renewables were not as successful as the Commission hoped. According to the 2009 Progress Report (EC 2009), the results were uneven among member states and several infringement procedures were opened, even though it was noted that progress had accelerated in more recent years.

By 2009, however, the intellectual and political climate in Europe had changed. In the early days, the promotion of renewables had been perceived as something of a luxury. But, after the 2007 launch of the 20-20-20 package, the promotion of renewables became a defining hallmark of the EU's very identity. In a sense, many in the EU believed that it defined the difference between the EU and the rest of the world. It should be noted that – at the time – Europe was experiencing relatively high rates of economic growth (which made it willing to pay more for the luxury of renewables, which can be seen as an income elastic good). The EU was also suffering from increasing oil prices that made the argument for moving away from hydrocarbons appear stronger. Coal was widely regarded as a dirty fuel, and natural gas – the

---

3   In particular, large hydroelectric power did not grow much because a large share of its potential had already been exploited, and because local communities tend to oppose the construction of new, large dams.

cleaner alternative – had the stigma of exposing Europe to excessive dependency from foreign sources, most notably Russia. The implications of the shale gas and liquefied natural gas (LNG) revolutions were still to be understood. Another relevant feature of the time was that many (if not most) renewable technology producers were headquartered in Europe, in countries such as Germany, Denmark and Spain.

A wave of rhetorical warnings about Europe's 'energy security' contributed to making green energy subsidies welcome. By then, subsidised renewables accounted for a small share of total power generation, so they were not really perceived as a burden by consumers. For example, according to Eurobarometer (2008), 74 per cent of Europeans said they believed that protecting the environment should be a priority for their country, even if it affected economic growth.

The political conditions for a more radical policy approach were all there, and they were fulfilled.

The second renewable energy sources directive

It was under such favourable conditions that the second Directive (2009/28/EC) was adopted in 2009. According to the European Renewable Energy Council (an umbrella lobby group for renewable energies in Brussels, that went into voluntary liquidation in 2014):

> In terms of access to the grid, the RES Directive stipulates that Member States should develop transmission and distribution grid infrastructure, intelligent networks, storage facilities and the electricity system generally, so as to accommodate the further development of electricity production from renewable energy sources, which includes interconnection between Member States and between Member States and third countries. The RES Directive also encourages Member States to accelerate

authorisation procedures for grid infrastructure and to coordinate approval of grid infrastructure with administrative and planning procedures (article 16). Furthermore, Member States are required to grant either priority access or guaranteed access to the grid-system of electricity produced from RES, and also ensure that Transmission System Operators (TSOs) give priority to generating installations using RES when dispatching electricity. Finally, Member States may also, where relevant, consider extending existing gas network infrastructure to facilitate the integration of gas from RES.

As far as quantitative targets are concerned, the Directive sets an EU-wide target for renewables of 20 per cent of total consumption by end users and chooses 2020 as the date by which this is to be achieved. The Directive, coupled with changing conditions largely due to the recession, has undoubtedly been effective. The recession caused energy demand to collapse. Prices fell accordingly in most member states. But renewables – most notably solar power, which is often subsidised through feed-in tariffs – were not subject to price signals because of the mechanism of subsidy. Because of guaranteed access and priority in dispatch, they also did not perceive any reduction in demand. Investment in renewables continued and capacity grew, despite general economic contraction, to the point that several EU member states overshot their interim targets in 2010 (EC 2013a,b). They continued to overshoot in the following years, as Figure 6 shows.

Overall, the EU is on track to meet, or exceed, its 2020 targets. In 2012, renewable power production at the EU level was as high as 62.5 MToe, just 2.8 per cent below the interim target. However, if one looks at this in retrospect, what the Commission laments is that – in a time of generation overcapacity – too little additional renewable generation had been injected into the system. Connecting renewable sources to the grid may have a huge cost, because, for example, the most windy or sunny locations can be far away from the main network, or from the places where energy is consumed (a case in point being offshore wind power). Moreover, intermittent production is also associated with other grid costs.

Figure 6 Renewable energy as a share of electricity generation compared with 2010 plans ('target')

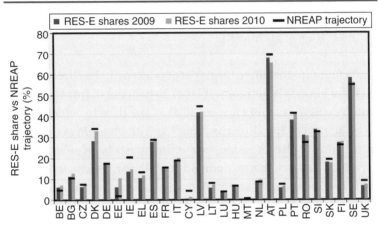

Source: EC (2013b). NREAP stands for National Renewable Energy Action Plans.

10 ENVIRONMENTAL REGULATION – ACHIEVING CARBON REDUCTION AT A HIGH COST

A number of renewable support schemes have been introduced across the EU (see Figure 7). These schemes were, on balance, effective at meeting their own interim goals (and the 2020 targets are very likely to be met). However, there is little evidence that they were efficient. In other words, it is likely that greenhouse gas output has been reduced at too high a cost. To put it another way, for a given cost, greenhouse gas output could have been reduced by more.

The EU does not provide a harmonised account of the aggregate amount of subsidies that are awarded annually by member states. However, a prima facie look at the difference between the levels of subsidies in different countries suggests that national lobbies have been more successful in grabbing rents than in achieving environmental benefits. This confirms the prediction of Helm (2009) that 'climate change ... is likely to be one of the largest sources of economic rents from policy interventions. There is a large and growing climate change "pork-barrel". It is highly unlikely that the policy costs will be zero. Indeed, there are good reasons to suppose otherwise – at every level of climate change policy'.

The cost of renewable support schemes

The introduction of widespread and often very generous support schemes for renewables has also caused significant costs to

Figure 7   Main renewable energy support instruments in the EU27

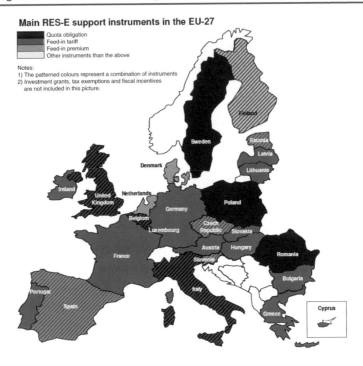

Main RES-E support instruments in the EU-27

Quota obligation
Feed-in tariff
Feed-in premium
Other instruments than the above

Notes:
1) The patterned colours represent a combination of instruments
2) Investment grants, tax exemptions and fiscal incentives
are not included in this picture.

Source: Ecofys (2011).

be imposed on consumers, who often fund such schemes. The Council of European Energy Regulators (CEER 2013) submitted a questionnaire to the EU member states; it was only completed by 17 of them. In 2010, the latest year for which data are available, around 277 TWh (which is equivalent to 9.3 per cent of gross energy production, or 10.7 per cent of final consumption) were awarded subsidies worth over €25 billion. The average level of support was €6.4/MWh with reference to end consumers (with a weighted average of €8.5/MWh).

The distribution of financial support is uneven both across countries and between technologies. On average, Spanish electricity consumers were most heavily hit. They paid €17.7 per consumed MWh in order to subsidise green energies (in turn, green generators took an average of as much as €88 per MWh that they produced). At the other end of the spectrum stands Finland, with an average levy of just €0.2 per MWh on consumers, corresponding to an average subsidy for the recipients of €6.1 per MWh.

The most subsidised technology was photovoltaics. They received €496/MWh in the Czech Republic and slightly lower subsidies in Belgium, France, Italy and Luxembourg. The least subsidised technologies were biogas and waste. In Finland, for example, they received a subsidy of €2.76/MWh.

It is virtually impossible to evaluate the effectiveness and efficiency of the renewable support schemes due to a lack of data. It is, nevertheless, possible to infer some qualitative judgements from these observations and from official reports by several European regulators.

The most striking case is that of solar power. Traditionally, this has been one of the less competitive renewable sources, but it enjoyed favourable conditions after 2010 due to a combination of factors. Eastern producers (most notably China) came into the market and offered low-cost panels. A few European countries (most notably Germany, Spain and Italy) awarded generous solar subsidies. The most attractive markets (i.e. those in which the highest incentives relative to cost were provided) were flooded by solar investment and installed capacity boomed. Even after the most recent cuts in subsidy, photovoltaics enjoyed by far the most generous incentives (Ecofys 2014).

The result was not only a massive flow of subsidies that contributed to increasing the cost of energy, but also a number of technical and economic problems related to network imbalances. These problems had and have a major impact on competition and power-market design, as costs are not always allocated in an efficient way, and economic agents behave (rationally) in perverse or opportunistic ways. Overall, the approach of subsidising different technologies to a different extent and providing different levels of subsidy in different countries has led to serious problems in electricity markets. Put simply, the cheapest ways of cutting carbon emissions have not been chosen.

A new framework has been introduced for 2030 which, whilst being more pragmatic than the previous 2020 package, mixes environmental and industrial policy goals.

Directives pulling in opposite directions

In summary, the EU passed two comprehensive sets of directives and other regulatory measures. One was aimed at opening national electricity markets and promoting market integration at the EU level. The other was aimed at reducing carbon emissions and promoting the deployment of a significant share of renewable generating capacity. These two sets of measures worked against each other. The liberalisation package was supposed to decentralise investment risk and decision-making so that the technologies chosen to generate power would reflect costs, demand and supply. Under such a framework, regulation should be focused on dealing with the transition from vertically integrated monopolies to competitive markets, and on the management of the essential facilities. However, in reality, obligations and regulations were introduced that significantly constrained the market's freedom to make investment decisions. Renewables obligations also distorted the pricing system and created a number of negative externalities, additional costs that were largely socialised. In a nutshell, what the liberalisation package was supposed to deliver was endangered by the obligations under the climate package. The climate change package was consistent with an approach guided by a 'government knows best' philosophy, rather than an approach whereby the government sets the rules but the actual decisions are made by firms and households.

PART 4

ELECTRICITY LIBERALISATION VERSUS CLIMATE INTERVENTIONISM

The problem created by dispersed information consists not in the circumstance that those who possess some relevant items of information are ignorant of the complementary items of information, but that they are ignorant of their ignorance ... This kind of unknown ignorance, when confronted by central planners, cannot be systematically or deliberately tackled. Planners simply do not know what to look for: they do not know where or of what kind the knowledge gaps are. And it is precisely this knowledge problem that the decentralized market economy addresses ... It turns out, then, that individual liberty is not merely one element in the definition of a market economy. It turns out that individual liberty is that ingredient in that definition upon which the success of the market process depends. Individual liberty is not a circumstance in spite of which markets work; it is the crucial circumstance which permits the market process to work.

Israel M. Kirzner (1992: 52–53)

11 DISTORTIONS FROM SUBSIDIES FOR RENEWABLES

The interaction of the EU's liberalisation and climate change policies is complex to say the least – the implementation of one policy has made it more difficult to reach the goals implied by the other. This is not about the purpose or goals of the policy – there is no contradiction in principle between achieving more competitive power markets and reducing carbon emissions. The problem lies entirely with the instruments that have been chosen to achieve the end of reducing carbon emissions. Climate policies and renewable subsidies risk jeopardising electricity markets by creating price distortions (different ways of reducing carbon emissions are mispriced), quantity distortions (investments in new generating capacity are no longer driven by expectations about demand and price patterns) and quality distortions (overinvestment in the favoured technologies occurs while investments in other technologies are crowded out). These distortions are discussed below and in the following chapters.

These distortions have been largely ignored. This was partly because they were small to begin with. In addition, increasing oil prices created the perception that decarbonisation had become relatively cheaper. On top of all this, demand was growing at such a fast pace that many thought it would absorb any additional capacity with little or no trouble.

This changed with the economic crisis and the subsequent collapse of electricity demand. Price distortions became greater because the same aggregate cost of subsidy was spread across a reduced level of consumption. The quantity distortion became more harmful as the share of the highly regulated renewable sector increased. The quality distortion was also made worse due to the imbalances between demand and supply for energy, which might have been more easily absorbed by a larger market, becoming problematic, as electricity production and intermittent sources of energy grew in absolute and relative terms. This meant that the relative burden of reserve capacity that had to be preserved to ensure the continual security of supply increased disproportionately.

Price distortions

Each EU member state has adopted its own schemes to promote renewables. The outturn in each country depends on the comparative advantage of each country in producing energy in different ways, often determined by natural characteristics (such as exposure to the sun, wind patterns, geothermal resources, etc.) and on the policy environment. The latter is heavily influenced by industry lobbying.

Industry capture

Institutional experimentation is usually a good thing, although in this case it was generally driven by common objectives, which relied both on binding targets set at the EU level and the very strong political pressures from environmentalist movements and governments captured by industry. The idea that average incomes would grow indefinitely (and energy demand increase accordingly), and that oil prices would also rise, driving natural gas prices up, contributed to the creation of a favourable investment and political climate for subsidised renewables.

Table 2 summarises the variety of instruments that have been adopted. It also shows that different tools have been employed

Table 2   Overview of RES electricity support instruments by country and technology

Member state	Hydro	Wind	Biomass and waste	Biogas	Photovoltaic	Geothermal
Austria	IGs, FiT	FiT	FiT	FiT	IGs, FiT	FiT
Belgium	GCs with GMP	GCs with GMP	GCs with GMP	GCs with GMP	GCs with GMP	GCs with GMP
Czech Republic	FiT, FiP	FiT, FiP	FiT, FiP	FiT, FiP	FiT, FiP	FiT, FiP
Estonia	FiP	FiP	FiP	FiP		
Finland	ETR	ETR	ETR	ETR		
France	FiT	FiT, CfT	FiT, CfT	FiT	FiT, CfT	FiT
Germany	FiT, DM, FiP	FiT, DM, FiP		FiT, DM, FiP	FiT, DM, FiP	FiT, DM, FiP
Hungary	FiT	FiT	FiT	FiT	FiT	FiT
Italy	GCs, FiTs	GCs, FiTs	GCs, FiTs	GCs, FiTs	FiT, FiP	GCs, FiTs
Lithuania	FiT	FiT	FiT	FiT	FiT	
Luxembourg	FiT, FiP	FiT, FiP		FiT, FiP	FiT, FiP	
Netherlands	FiP	FiP	FiP		FiP	
Portugal	FiT	FiT, Tendering process	FiT, Tendering process	FiT	FiT	FiT
Romania	GCs	GCs	GCs	GCs	GCs	
Slovenia	FiT	FiT	FiT	FiT	FiT	
Spain	FiT or FiP (optional)	FiT or FiP (optional)	FiT or FiP (optional)	FiT or FiP (optional)	FiT (PV) and FiT or FiP (CSP)	
UK	GC, FiT	GC, FiT	GCs		GCs, FiT	

CfT, call for tenders; DM, direct marketing; ETR, Excise tax return; FiP, feed-in premium; FiT, feed-in tariff; GC, green certificate; GMP, guaranteed minimum price; IG, investment grant.
Source: CEER (2013).

to support different technologies. The simultaneous adoption of so many policy tools is inconsistent with the nature of the single objective of reducing carbon emissions. Instead, this approach to policy reflects industrial policy objectives that have little to do with achieving environmental goals in the most cost-effective way.

Figure 8   Average support to renewable energy production in
the EU [€/MWh] by country

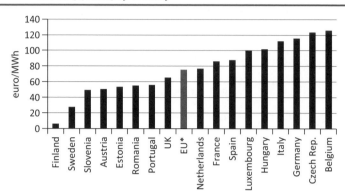

*The average involves only the countries that are listed in this figure.
Source: CEER (2013) with additional details from the author.

There have been many different approaches to supporting renewables, and the extent to which they were used varied between countries and energy types as well as over time. This has led to significant variation both in the cost of the renewable programmes and in the cost of CO_2 abatement policies. There is no clear economic case for providing different subsidies for different technologies. With the partial exception of concentrated solar power (CSP), no major renewable technology can be defined as an 'infant' technology, and thus, even if one accepts the infant industry argument for subsidies, it is not generally valid in the case of renewable technologies. Since the environmental benefit of one extra unit of renewable, carbon-free energy is the same regardless of the technology employed, there is no rationale from an environmental perspective for granting different subsidies to different technologies. Doing so simply reduces the extent of carbon abatement for a given cost.

Figure 8 shows how subsidies vary across states, and Figure 9 shows how they vary across technologies averaged across states.

Figure 9 Average support to renewable energy production in the EU(€/MWh) by technology

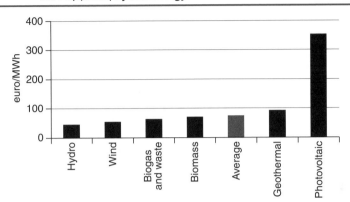

*The average involves only the countries that are listed in Figure 8.
Source: CEER (2013) with additional details from the author.

The heterogeneity in the support given to renewable energy sources suggests that the incentives were set with little or no regard for their environmental benefit; otherwise, one would expect no difference between technologies (because the environmental benefit of each carbon-free MWh is the same).

Costs of renewable energy production in different countries

One useful exercise is to estimate the CO_2 abatement costs related to renewable energy production in different countries. Eurelectric (2012) provides data for the level of emissions from power generation in each country. This allows us to estimate the average per unit emissions from conventional power generation. By dividing total expenditure on green subsidies by the reduction in emissions caused by renewables displacing conventional technologies, we have a first-order estimate of the average cost of abatement per tonne of CO_2 (see Figure 11). This varies hugely

Figure 10 Average CO$_2$ abatement cost in some EU member states

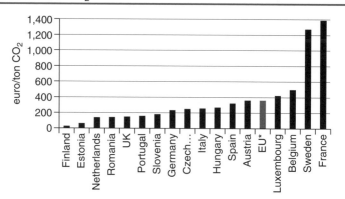

*The European average involves only the countries that are listed in this figure.
Source: CEER (2013) and Eurelectric (2012) with details added by the author.

across countries. These figures are calculated by assuming that the conventional plants displaced by renewable generation emit at the average for all plants, and, thus, they do not perfectly capture the cost of carbon abatement at the margin. In fact, the marginal abatement cost is likely to be underestimated in most cases.

Figure 10 shows the results of the analysis.

The cost of abating CO$_2$ emissions by means of renewables is very high. Even in Finland – the EU member state that invests the least in green subsidies – €27 has been paid, on average, per tonne of CO$_2$ abated, well above the market value of emission allowances in the European Emissions Trading Scheme (which oscillates between €5–10/tonne CO$_2$ at the time of writing). It should be noted that the marginal cost of abating CO$_2$ is very high in France and Sweden, because these countries rely on low-emitting generation fleets (based on nuclear power in the former country, and nuclear and hydropower in the latter). Therefore, at the margin, the amount of avoided emissions is very low because renewables displace low-carbon technologies. This provides a clear example of how the juxtaposition of competing targets – such as those related to emissions reductions and renewables promotion – may lead to contradictory outcomes. It would be far better for renewables to be used to a greater degree in countries other than France and Sweden, as well as less in France and Sweden themselves, but EU directives prevent that.

The irrational outcome of renewables policies

Something is clearly very wrong with the policy of promoting renewables. A carbon emissions target has been set by the EU, which has an emission trading scheme designed for the purpose of meeting the target. Under that scheme, firms are willing to accept around €5–10 to reduce CO_2 output by one tonne. However, on average EU governments are willing to pay as much as €362 per tonne of CO_2 abated. This is an extremely large discrepancy and suggests that EU energy policy is encouraging the reduction in carbon output through methods that are far more expensive than necessary.

The other outcome of large subsidies relates to the price formation mechanism. The electricity price is the sum of three components: an unregulated component (that reflects the market price of electricity as a commodity),[1] a regulated component (that includes network costs, renewable subsidies and so on), and taxes. The market price of electricity as a commodity has recently been pushed down by a reduction in natural gas prices, the recession-driven collapse in demand and European liberalisation, which all created the conditions for more competition.

Indeed, the subsidy grew dramatically as the amount of deployed, green capacity increased. Therefore, a larger amount of money has been taken from consumers through an increase

---

1   Generally speaking, at any given point in time, and for any given level of demand, the wholesale price of electricity reflects the marginal cost of the marginal generator.

in the regulated part of the electricity price. This phenomenon was magnified by the demand reduction, which correspondingly increased the burden of subsidies per unit of consumption so that prices increased disproportionately. As a consequence, variations in wholesale prices became smoothed as they were passed on to end consumers, who barely perceived changes in wholesale prices because of the corresponding increase in the regulated part of the price designed to subsidise renewables. As a result, the end consumer did not perceive any benefit from liberalisation. The fact that prices would have been lower if liberalisation had been pursued without the renewables policies adding to the bills is a complex argument for consumers to follow. The political-economy case for liberalisation was undermined as a result of the benefits being masked by the renewables policies.

This interference in the price mechanism led, from a competition standpoint, to two major consequences. Firstly, the consumer was less able to perceive price variations over time and, hence, less able to adjust their behaviour to market signals. Secondly, the consumer was also less able to perceive the difference between commercial offers from competing producers, so market behaviour became more sticky and the propensity to switch to an alternative supplier was reduced.

Both effects made competition less effective by discouraging more active demand-side behaviour.

Quantity distortions

As well as renewables being given monetary support, European directives mandate that they are given guaranteed access to the grid or priority dispatch. A consequence of the combination of these features is that green generators are highly insensitive to market signals. As long as green generation is lower than total demand, there is virtually no volume risk, because the system operator is required to accept any extra unit of green energy as it is produced (or to compensate generators if it is not possible to deliver the energy). As far as prices are concerned, regulated tariffs or other mechanisms (such as those based on green certificates or tax breaks) are designed in such a way that it is advantageous for the generator to sell its energy, even if its market value is close to or below zero. So, price risk is almost absent for any practical purpose. The state has, in effect, guaranteed prices for renewable energy, regardless of what happens to the price of other forms of energy.

In the absence of demand and price risks, supply is only limited by physical factors such as the development time for new facilities and the availability of physical connections to the power grid. It is therefore not surprising that there has been a huge increase in green energy. Whilst total demand for energy was growing, the crowding out of conventional supply was limited. Indeed, in most European countries there was a feeling that either total capacity was scarce relative to potential demand, or that it would become scarce over a short period of time. Power plants were running at high loads and margins were high, even though there was a growing perception of political risk due to the continual interference by government (HSBC 2012).

Then the economic crisis came, and the scenario abruptly changed. To put it in very simple terms, until 2009, there was room for everybody in the power market. After 2009, with the fall of GDP across Europe and the subsequent reduction in electricity demand, especially from large, industrial consumers, generators found themselves in a much more competitive situation, and it was more difficult to recover fixed costs. However, it was not the most expensive generation capacity that was retired, as this was subsidised. Furthermore, the contestable part of the market – i.e. the part of the demand that generators compete with each other to supply – shrank, leaving a much bigger renewable sector that is not open to competition.

Figure 11 Share of renewable and non-renewable electricity production in EU28

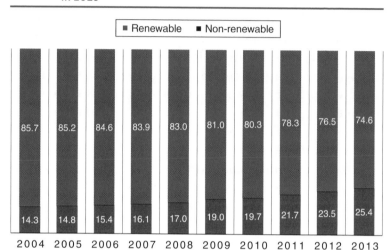

Source: Eurostat

Figure 11 shows the extent of the contraction of the contestable part of the market over time.

Renewable production increased steadily over time, while non-renewable generation first grew moderately and then decreased by entirely absorbing the reduction in total demand. Between 2008 (when the crisis exploded) and 2012, the amount of electricity consumption covered by renewable sources grew from 487 TWh to 657 TWh, while conventional generation shrunk from 2,378 TWh to 2,139 TWh.

The reduction in size of the contestable part of the market is even more significant than this. The non-contestable portion of the market is not limited to green, subsidised generation: if network constraints, reserve margins and the production time profile are taken into account, the situation is worse.

The costs of reserve capacity

Network constraints relate to limits on the ability of power grids to convey energy as would happen if it could move freely from any generating point to any consumer. At the national level – and even more so at the EU level – many inefficient plants are employed and much pollution is produced because the capacity of the electricity lines is not sufficient for the available power. In many cases, network investments are either in progress or planned, but these constraints are still relevant. These problems have little to do with renewables as such, but, in practice, renewables create an additional problem.

Reserve capacity is designed to deal with intermittent generation. As we saw in Chapter 3, the power system needs to be kept in constant, real-time equilibrium. Conventional energy sources, as well as programmable renewables (the production of which does not depend on the sun or wind), do not usually create problems. On average, they produce the required amount of energy (which is set, for example, on the day-ahead market) at the planned time. But with sources such as solar and wind power, things are very different. There can be long periods of cloud or periods without wind, often at a time when power demand will be great.[2] Some approximate forecasting is possible, but production can change rapidly and without notice. If such deviations from forecasts are not to disrupt the system, some reserve capacity must be kept in operation.

For reserve capacity to be available, power plants providing the reserve must be producing at least at their technical minimum capacity – that is, some power is being injected into the system. This is necessary, because in order for power from a generator to be increased, the generating capacity must be running at a given minimum level. This energy must have priority on the grid too.

2   In the UK, for example, cold winters are often very still.

The amount of reserve capacity has been estimated at around 20–25 per cent of the amount of intermittent capacity that is available at any given point in time. For a thermal unit to provide quick reserve when needed, it should be operated at around 40 per cent of its nominal capacity (for further discussion of the issue and an empirical analysis of the consequences of intermittent generation, see, for example, Korchinski (2013)). This is further power that is not subject to the normal functioning of the market but is subject to regulatory command.

Because intermittent capacity has grown rapidly in the past few years, there may be times of the day when the entire demanded load is covered either by intermittent capacity or reserve capacity. That may be the case for night-time demand in Nordic countries, when offshore wind power is producing at close to full capacity, or it may be the case in summer in southern European countries, when solar power is at full capacity. At these times, the idle reserve capacity has to be remunerated, and the cost of capital certainly has to be borne. This adds hidden costs to the visible cost of green subsidies.

Quality distortions

Demand and supply imbalances with intermittent generation

Intermittent generators create an imbalance problem whenever the divergence between actual and forecasted generation becomes too wide. Adequate incentives should be set in order to minimise such deviations. The goal of balancing demand and supply can be reached, by and large, through ad hoc regulation that charges intermittent generators for the cost of the imbalances they cause. Several EU member states have adopted such provisions. Yet, the cost of imbalances may grow more than proportionately to the amount of intermittent generation.[3] When the intermittent capacity is small, the cost of imbalances is small and can be easily absorbed by the system. When intermittent capacity grows beyond a given level, however, it may become unsustainable.

Yet, one consequence of renewable subsidies is that they partly or totally shield intermittent generators from paying for the negative externalities they impose on the system. Indeed, the cost of such externalities is mostly passed onto conventional, unsubsidised generators and, eventually, consumers. As a consequence, in the absence of specific corrections (that may or may not be consistent with the broader liberalisation framework) problems grow larger and larger, with more and more subsidised capacity being added to the system, and conventional generators being crowded out. This is what can be called the 'quality distortion'.

There are several reasons for this. One is the above-discussed issue of reserve capacity, which creates an artificial need for the fixed, sunk costs of such capacity to be borne by consumers. Another is that network congestion can become pathological and may require the availability of additional spinning reserve. Finally, intermittent generation also has a major effect on the way prices are formed in the wholesale markets, as well as on the margins of conventional generators that, in turn, may adapt their lobbying activity.

As we saw in Chapter 5, most wholesale markets are based upon a 'system marginal price' rule: each generator bids in a power exchange at its marginal cost of generation, and bids are ordered in ascending order, while offer prices are ordered the other way around. Supply and demand curves will match at the equilibrium.

---

3   It may be possible to keep the costs lower if renewable generators are very well distributed across a country, and if the power grid is so robust and well interconnected that each site's deviation from the expected generation profile can be offset by pooling it with other sites' deviations in the opposite direction.

The equilibrium price is equivalent to the marginal generation cost of the marginal generator for any given couple of demand and supply curves; so, any other generator gains a margin that is equal to the difference between its own marginal cost and the market-clearing price (the so-called inframarginal rent). Inframarginal rents are supposed to be high enough for generating companies to recover their fixed costs as well as make an acceptable return on invested capital.

What happens when subsidised capacity comes into play, and what is the subsidised generators' bidding strategy? The answer is straightforward: the marginal generation cost for wind and solar stations is zero (or below zero), while for other renewables it is relatively low or negative. Even if marginal costs are higher than zero, they have priority on the grid. This means that they 'enter' the market by displacing – or shifting rightwards in the merit order curve – conventional production. Subsequently the market-clearing price falls.

This effect is known as 'peak shaving' from green sources: power prices at peak time are significantly cut because of green generation. The peak-shaving effect can be very great under appropriate conditions, especially if prices are left free to fall below zero when renewable generation is very large relative to the quantities demanded, and if there are also conventional plants that for some reason cannot be shut off (Benedettini and Stagnaro 2014).

This may sound like it is good for consumers, but in fact there are unpleasant consequences.

The first consequence is that the usual peak price does not disappear, nor is it lowered as much as one would expect. Rather, it is shifted in time. Solar panels, in particular, produce a huge amount of energy in the middle of the day, when solar radiation is at its maximum. But, as the sun goes down, solar production falls quickly. The system needs to stay in equilibrium. Demand also peaks in the middle of the day but falls slowly. Baseload plants – those power plants that are designed to work virtually without interruption – are then not sufficient to match demand. Conventional power plants, therefore, must ramp up their production very fast, starting from their technical minimum. As a conventional power plant is put into motion, or when its output is required to grow quickly, its marginal generation cost tends to be higher. The opposite problem occurs earlier in the morning, when solar production rapidly increases and conventional generation is supposed to abruptly reduce output.

The result of this is that the usual pattern of power prices – with a peak around noon when demand is at its highest – changes shape, turning into a two-peaked pattern with a mid-morning peak, another in the late afternoon and a minimum around the middle of the day. Figure 12 shows an example.

The difference between the two patterns is self-evident. Both panels in Figure 12 show the hourly price of electricity for the Sicily market zone in Italy on a Wednesday in mid-May but in two different years, 2010 and 2014. There was a major difference between the two years in the amount of subsidised, intermittent energy sources, particularly solar power.

Wind power has similar results, though they are less predictable.

Renewables, priority access and competition distortions

This also creates room for opportunistic, albeit not necessarily illegal, market behaviours, and it results in the possibility of anticompetitive outcomes. These surges in prices can also be magnified because of tacit collusion (Ivaldi et al. 2003) among market actors. While anti-competition authorities are supposed to prevent or punish such behaviours, they are very difficult to spot. They are, of course, the result of regulatory choices, such as subsidies, guaranteed grid access and priority dispatch.

All producers know that in the late afternoon solar production will fall and conventional production will have to ramp up (although nobody knows the precise time and quantities involved).

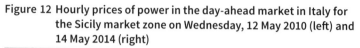

Figure 12 Hourly prices of power in the day-ahead market in Italy for the Sicily market zone on Wednesday, 12 May 2010 (left) and 14 May 2014 (right)

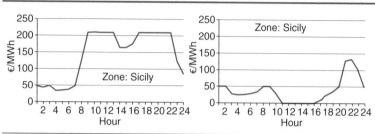

Conventional generators have a common interest in pushing up the marginal price during the transition hours, in order to earn higher margins and increase the probability of recovering their own fixed costs. So, there may be an incentive to shut off the least costly power plants (those usually employed in baseload generation) in order to reduce supply and raise the prices that will be received as the more costly plants are brought into production. Since there is a common interest in doing so, tacit collusion may occur. This is hard to expose as illegitimate behaviour, because it may well be a rational response to the conditions, given the small number of generators that will be supplying the market in this situation, and given that the size of the contestable market has been reduced by the subsidisation of renewables that have priority access to the grid.

Furthermore, when solar production is at its peak, even though demand is also at its maximum, the size of the contestable market is very small. If renewable generation (which has a delivery priority) and the bulk of baseload generation (which it would be uneconomical to shut off) are added together, there is very little room for marginal generators to compete with each other. This does not merely result in the kind of opportunistic behaviours that have been described above, but also reduces the incentive to, and expected payoff from, entry. So, the scope for potential, as well as actual, competition is narrowed. The net effect on the consumer's welfare may be ambiguous. On the one hand, prices at peak times (when the demanded volumes are the highest) are lower than without renewables; on the other hand, off-peak prices are higher, and additional costs (such as the cost of imbalances, the cost of additional reserve capacity and the cost of subsidies) are embedded in the power bill. The quality of the electricity production process is damaged by these problems. It is not so much that the consumer notices a substantial difference but that the generation process becomes inefficient as it becomes less and less cost- and demand-reflective. The paradox of subsidies is that they result in lower prices when demand peaks, and higher prices when demand falls; of course, this affects demand itself, creating an incentive for consumers to demand more at peak times and less and less thereafter. Investors as well as grid operators are sent the wrong signals and act accordingly, making the situation even worse and crowding out 'market-based' investments while rewarding rent-seekers. Subsidy-oriented investments are privileged over those investments that are genuinely exposed to market risks. This is exactly the opposite of a market failure: it is the consequence of rational market behaviours under dysfunctional rules.

As we shall see, a further reason why subsidised generation increases costs and reduces competition is that it makes politically stronger the case for introducing capacity remuneration mechanisms that reward generators for the development of capacity rather than for generation itself. The movement from energy-only markets to markets that remunerate energy and capacity, in turn, was accelerated in the EU by the recession-driven collapse of power demand in a time of growing subsidised installed capacity.

12 THE NEW WORLD OF OVERCAPACITY

The tensions and problems in the market described above remained latent whilst demand was growing. Then, the recession came, and all the problems were suddenly exacerbated. The cost of renewables fell more rapidly than the subsidies, so investment in subsidised capacity boomed instead of slowing down. By the time generous subsidies were cut down to more reasonable levels, the 'perfect storm' created by subsidies, low-cost technologies and falling demand had already hit the EU.

As a consequence, the fall in demand for electricity has been completely absorbed by conventional power generators, as shown by Figure 13.

Until 2008, installed capacity as well as total demand grew. But, after the economic crisis, the trends of demand and installed capacity became decoupled: demand decreased sharply, whilst supply kept growing, mostly driven by subsidised, renewable capacity. Between 2008 and 2011, total demand in the EU28 decreased by 2.6 per cent, while non-renewable installed capacity increased by 3.7 per cent (mostly because of previously planned investments); renewable capacity, excluding hydropower, more than doubled (with solar photovoltaic rising by 349 per cent).

The average utilisation factor of conventional power plants – i.e. the ratio between their potential output and their actual production – decreased accordingly. Since renewable energy has grid priority over non-renewables in most member states, the load reduction fell entirely upon conventional capacity, which

Figure 13 Installed generating capacity by source (bars, left axis) versus final electricity consumption (line, right axis) in the EU28

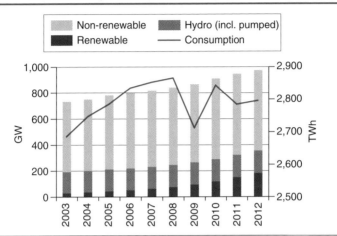

also absorbed the partial reduction of prices connected with the 'peak shaving' effect (Pepermans et al. 2005; Toledo et al. 2010). In other words, conventional generators – which were accustomed to a relatively comfortable rate of return on their own investments – entered the world of overcapacity.

In most industries, overcapacity leads to plant closures. This may (and sometimes does) happen in the power sector too, but there are at least two complicating factors. The first is the need for spare capacity to be maintained in order to build up the reserve margin that is necessary to balance the system in the presence of large intermittent production. The higher the intermittent generation, the higher the required reserve margin, all else being equal. Paradoxically, the growth of subsidised intermittent generation leads to a requirement for conventional generators to remain in use to provide back-up capacity. However, the fact that their use will only be necessary under certain circumstances makes it more difficult for them to cover their fixed costs: the lower the need for conventional plants under normal circumstances, the harder it is to meet the fixed costs of providing this additional generating capacity when it is essential.

The second complicating factor is that, in most EU member states, the incumbents and several smaller companies are owned (or controlled) by the state or local governments. As always, government ownership makes adjustments more difficult and politically costly (McKenzie 1984; OECD 2010; Scarpa et al. 2010; Bortolotti et al. 2011).

The expected future growth in renewables will result in a further major growth of capacity that cannot be brought into action simply to meet demand (for example, because the wind is not blowing). Such capacity in the EU is forecast to increase from about 250 GW in 2013 to almost 600 GW in 2030. The power industry is likely to suffer both from overcapacity as well as political interference in the restructuring process. This is not a healthy combination in a market where long-term decisions have to be made and the fixed costs of production are high.

In the absence of political interference, even with the subsidisation of intermittent technology, balancing markets (or other mechanisms) should provide adequate incentives for maintaining otherwise uneconomical plants. Even when a facility is used at a very low level compared with its potential capacity, if the price paid for the flexibility it provides is high enough, it may be able to cover its variable as well as fixed costs. Given the existence of subsidised renewables, the only question is the price that is necessary to bring into play further capacity, including covering fixed costs, when demand is greater than supply.

Well-developed markets provide robust instruments to assess the real need for a plant to be kept operating, for example, through price signals from futures markets (Kiesling 2008) or via 'scarcity rents' (i.e. higher and higher prices, as supply is not likely to keep the real-time pace of demand growth). If bringing into play additional supply is not economical given the fixed costs, mechanisms for passing through prices that reflect scarcity at different times of day to consumers and reducing demand can be developed (such as smart metering). Well-functioning retail markets can be very helpful in this, but they presuppose that prices reflect costs: subsidies may and do result in the decoupling of marginal generation costs from actual prices, so consumers may not perceive what is going on and may react in ways that, albeit rational to them, exacerbate the supply-side problems already discussed.

With regard to political interference, closing unprofitable power plants, especially when unemployment is high, may lead to difficulties.

A dangerous, but increasingly invoked, solution to these problems is the introduction of so-called capacity remuneration mechanisms (CRMs). These are financial schemes that pay power companies for the capacity that they provide, rather than for the energy they produce. These schemes can allow politicians to avoid the difficult decisions necessary when plants have to be closed, because such plants can be used to provide spare capacity to deal with imbalances between supply and demand caused by the use of renewables. However, these capacity mechanisms come at a cost.

13 CAPACITY SUPPORT SCHEMES: THE WRONG ANSWER

Do markets under-supply reliability?

Proposals for state-regulated or subsidised support schemes undermine the fundamental functions of the market. The basic question is this: for any given level of system reliability, who is best informed to make a meaningful decision about how much available capacity is needed? Furthermore, what is the optimum level of reliability? Reliability has a cost, and the greater the reliability, the greater the cost in terms of keeping capacity in reserve. In other words, there is a trade-off between reliability and cost.

The information about cost and benefits is dispersed among market actors, and we need competitive markets so that the price system can drive investment decisions. As in other markets, different suppliers will provide products with different levels of quality, with one dimension of quality in this case being reliability of supply. Alternatively, it could be argued that regulators have the best available information and, hence, should be made responsible for setting long-term targets for investment in spare capacity that might overcome the problems of the alleged 'short-sightedness' of market agents. This is essentially the view that is taken in many EU countries, including (but not limited to) the UK, France, Germany, Italy, Spain and Poland, where capacity remuneration schemes (i.e. CRMs) are either operational or under consideration.

A variety of policy tools can be used for financing the spare capacity (see IEFE 2013 for a classification of them; see also Batlle and Rodilla 2010 and Cramton and Ockenfelds 2011). The tools range from those that set regulated target quantities and prices for electricity to those that are designed in more market-friendly ways (such as 'capacity markets', where the required capacity is auctioned).

All such schemes, though, have a distinctive factor in common: the assumption that pure market signals would lead to the underprovision of capacity, down to a level that makes the system unreliable. Therefore, it is argued that a regulator has to set a given level of capacity that must be made available and maintained in the long run in case of shortages caused by intermittent forms of generation. This is done even though it appears that consumers are not freely willing to pay for the cost of maintaining the systems in order to maintain the spare capacity, because they do not value the additional reliability as being worth the cost.

The main argument for establishing a capacity support scheme is the so-called missing money problem (see, for example, Ausubel and Cramton 2010; Meunier 2010; Rious et al. 2012). In practice, market design or the industrial structure may cause the generators' revenues to be insufficient to finance the optimal level of investments. If investments are suboptimal, spare capacity will be insufficient to guarantee the desired level of system reliability. The increase of intermittent generation has made the problem much bigger.

The problem is not with the market as such. Under particular legal or regulatory arrangements, the price system may not be able to deliver the incentives to finance the optimal level of investment. Yet, such deficiencies are most likely to arise from regulation. The basic problem is that politicians believe that, in times of temporary shortages of supply, the resulting prices would be 'too high' and politically unacceptable, and, therefore, that they should not be permitted (see Stagnaro and Testa 2013 for an example from Italy). Hence, beyond a certain level, the demand side would not receive the correct price signal to adjust to the scarcity, and the supply side would not be able to rely on price signals generating the revenue to finance investment. Those generators that provide spare capacity would not be sufficiently rewarded for doing so. As Cramton et al. (2013) argue:

> During rolling blackouts, essentially every generator is running, so all are paid the same high scarcity price. Typically, the price is capped too low. That means there is 'missing money,' which implies too low a level of investment in capacity. One key observation about missing money is that, since it is missing from scarcity hours, every generator is missing essentially the same amount of money per MW of capacity. There are two basic ways to restore the missing money in proportion to MW of capacity (so that this results in incentives for building the correct mix of generation technologies): (1) raise scarcity prices paid during blackouts (price-based approach), and (2) pay every supplier of capacity the same amount per MW of capacity (quantity-based approach).

While theoretically needed to solve a policy-induced problem, capacity support schemes offer a convenient and sometimes not very transparent tool for policymakers to subsidise traditional utilities, in order to help them escape the curse of overcapacity in the presence of high fixed costs. Among other possible criticisms, this neglects the evidence that consumers understand and accept that prices may occasionally spike (Moran and Skinner 2008). If they are confronted with the trade-off between lower average prices, which would result from less investment in generally idle capacity, and higher peak prices, versus the alternative of a higher average and lower peak prices, they are likely to prefer the former. This is a similar question to whether airline passengers would prefer higher average prices (with airlines having greater total capacity) or lower average prices with the possibility that at some peak times it may be impossible to get a flight, or flights may be extremely expensive. Of course, the preferences for smoothed electricity prices and reliability of supply may be different from those in the air-passenger market, but the principle is the same. And, in both cases, different suppliers can offer a different combination of reliability, price smoothness and average cost.

Instead of responding to the regulatory failure with further interventions in the market, the initial failure should be removed. Indeed, there is a two-stage government failure. The government has, in the first place, encouraged the use of intermittent sources of supply. It has then compounded this failure by preventing price signals from balancing the consequent fluctuating supply and demand in the market.

Second-best interventions

Assuming that the problem does in fact exist and that it cannot be removed in the short run (either for practical or for political reasons), there is a wide range of market-based arrangements that can address the issue of long-term generation adequacy, so that capacity mechanisms have only a residual role, if any (Roques 2008).

As noted above, the growth of intermittent generation, and the underlying systemic problems it produces, are not examples of what economists describe as 'market failures': these problems result from political choices. Renewable subsidies are a policy instrument that is predicated upon the need to reduce negative externalities from burning fossil fuels. Yet, they themselves generate negative externalities – intermittency. Therefore, by the same logic that requires fossil fuel externalities to become part of the cost of carbon-based sources, it seems logical that the cost of intermittency-related externalities is paid for by intermittent producers. If this is done, intermittency will not be 'overproduced'. Generators would then be able to choose between different renewable technologies, with the problem of intermittency being reflected in the cost base. How can such a situation be brought about? One common solution, which is being adopted or considered in several countries, is to charge intermittent generators the cost of the imbalances they cause. Although imperfect, this kind of mechanism sets the right incentives by inducing renewable operators to expend resources on forecasting their production profile in the most accurate way possible. An even better solution might be to develop balancing markets in such a way that the pricing of imbalances is not ultimately left to administrative decisions, but instead relies on a competitive assessment of the marginal cost of intermittency. However, even the best-functioning balancing market will hardly be able to fully internalise the external cost of intermittent renewables (Borenstein 2011).

Demand-side adjustments may well become more efficient than the provision of spare capacity as technology changes. This may happen through improved storage facilities (Acer 2014) or mechanisms that allow demand to adjust to fluctuating supply. Subsidising capacity schemes will undermine the development of alternative ways of addressing this problem.

Defects of capacity remuneration mechanisms

Capacity remuneration mechanisms suffer from various defects. The first is the potential for design imperfections. Those who design a CRM can only have a limited knowledge of the nature of the problem. The most comprehensive cost-benefit analysis cannot anticipate all possible costs and benefits, including dynamic effects, nor will it accurately reflect the cost of all externalities. In particular, it is very hard to take into account the long-term consequences of capacity support mechanisms. Firms may behave in an opportunistic or even perverse way because they receive the wrong incentives from the regulatory environment. For example, firms may be induced to over- or under-invest, conditions may be created for tacit collusion or a firm's market power could be increased by the combination of regulatory restraints on the behaviour of competitors and network congestion. Regulation always brings about offsetting behaviours (Peltzman 1975, 2010), which can even lead to an outcome that is the opposite of that intended. Whenever circumstances require more regulation, it is advisable to carefully heed the dynamic, rather than just the static, consequences.

The second problem pervades all regulatory interventions designed to improve on the workings of a market. As indicated above, the regulator – or whoever is in charge of solving the problem – simply does not know the 'optimum' outcome from the market that would have been achieved in the absence of the so-called failures in that market. The necessary information is always incomplete, both because it is costly to accumulate and because much of it is subjectively held by consumers. It is simply not possible for regulators to know consumers' preferences or the amount they would be willing to pay for a service that avoids intermittency and price spikes. In terms of the supply side, in order to determine the optimum amount of spare capacity, regulators would also need to know the following: the short- and long-run amount of capacity that is needed to balance the system; the required rate of return on investments (or other, equivalent regulatory measures) needed to meet that goal; the site- and time-specific conditions under which the operating reserve will be needed; the long-term, marginal social cost of pollution compared with the long-term marginal cost of pollution abatement arising from the combination of green generation and CRMs; the idiosyncratic and systematic risks of different investment plans; a perfect knowledge of looming technological advancements; future demand patterns; etc.

In short, markets are needed to discover relevant information relating to the costs and benefits of different levels of supply reliability and price smoothness as well as the different ways of providing it.

Finally, there is the problem of politics. In their seminal papers, Stigler (1971, 1974) and Peltzman (1976) showed that regulation cannot be safely assumed to maximise general welfare. Regulation is strongly influenced by the way the political process works, and there is a kind of path dependency in regulation. Even under the most favourable assumptions, regulation tends to increase the utility of some powerful vested interests, especially in a market such as electricity, which has a relatively small number of big companies involved. In this case, there are clearly two beneficiaries: renewable generators (who socialise, to some extent, the costs they impose on the system but also receive very generous subsidies) and conventional generators (which, as they are challenged by green generators, seek to offset this cost by obtaining payments for the capacity they provide, in addition to the energy they sell).

Capacity schemes in practice

A capacity scheme is in place, or is about to be introduced, in most EU member states. In most cases, the scheme that has been adopted is a capacity payment, i.e. a regulated payment that is provided to those generators that make available a given amount of capacity with specific characteristics. Most recently, some member states – notably France, Italy and the UK – have either introduced or reformed their capacity schemes by adopting a capacity market. This involves a reverse auction, whereby the regulator and/or the system operator sets a capacity target. Utilities are asked to bid a price to make the desired capacity available. The lowest bidders would be awarded the requested payment.

The cost of the CRM is a function of how much capacity is required as well as the mechanism design. The money to fund it, though, would eventually come from end users, who would be charged through an increase (all else being equal) in the regulated component of the electricity price. From a competition point of view, this would result in three major changes in the way electricity markets work.

- All else being equal, the regulated component of the price would grow relative to the unregulated component, thus shifting the balance of market influence away from supply-and-demand conditions to political considerations.

- On the supply side, the nature of the business would no longer be that of selling power to consumers based on their preferences but would involve selling capacity to a centralised buyer based on political decisions.

- On the demand side, the lower relevance of the unregulated component of the price would smooth the difference between alternative commercial offers, undermining the functioning of retail markets.

The experience of the first auction under the new British capacity market (which was held on 16 December 2014)[1] seemed to suggest that power systems may well survive even without capacity support schemes. The British scheme is particularly interesting because it fully complied with EU state-aid rules on non-discrimination and technology neutrality; it was a well-designed scheme, as far as capacity support mechanisms go, but it radically changed the nature of the market that was once the most successful model (although a capacity support scheme had been in place until 2000).

In the auction, the market cleared at a price very close to the government's estimate of the fixed operating and maintenance

---

1 www.gov.uk/government/uploads/system/uploads/attachment_data/file/389832/ Provisional_Results_Report-Ammendment.pdf.

costs of a typical combined cycle gas turbine. Unsurprisingly, 45 per cent of the auctioned capacity will be provided by such plants, while 68 per cent will be provided by existing plants – rather than plants that are being built for the purpose of providing spare capacity. As Benedettini (2014b) pointed out, this situation is still far from ideal. It means that such plants are using capacity remuneration as a tool to recover their fixed costs that cannot be covered by selling electricity in a distorted market. This leads to production levels that are too low during normal times. In addition, despite the emphasis on not favouring particular technologies, intermittent renewables are still far from competitive compared with conventional generators, especially when the need for capacity support is taken into account. In effect, conventional generation is being subsidised through the capacity support mechanism helping to cover fixed costs, a situation that only arises because of the intermittency of subsidised renewables. This is a vicious circle of policy intervention. De Meulemeester (2014) has summarised the problem of capacity support schemes as being an 'expensive solution for a non-existing problem'.

Even from an environmental point of view, the British capacity scheme may fail to deliver. Some have argued that the UK's capacity market works as a hidden subsidy to conventional (fossil and nuclear) generators (van Renssen 2014c), while others believe it is not a market at all (Parr 2015). The cost of the scheme is estimated to be around £1 billion per year, so concerns are well founded. On top of that, the British energy regulator opened an investigation into the behaviour of several companies, who may have misstated the terms in the bid. This latter argument is not, per se, an argument against the CRM in principle, but it suggests that such schemes require very close and strict monitoring.

The case for a CRM in the UK is even weaker, as the government has understood that most problems in the electricity market are not a result of market failures: rather, they are a consequence of subsidy-driven uneconomic investment. In fact, UK Energy and

Climate Secretary, Amber Rudd, announced that green subsidies would be cut because they are growing too costly to consumers and distort competition (Reed 2015).

Summing up, rather than being a technical mechanism designed to make markets work properly, CRMs appear to be policy tools that result in the recentralising of decision-making. They are not a solution for a problem, they are a further problem.

Providing capacity in the market

Conventional generators are being displaced by falling demand and the growing competitiveness of green technologies. To an extent, green technologies are becoming more competitive as a result of innovation and scientific progress: this is not a process simply driven by subsidy. Even if EU countries had technology-neutral approaches to reducing carbon emissions, it is likely that more intermittent generating capacity would be developed. In these circumstances, one might think of capacity support schemes as some sort of 'necessary evil' either to offset some of the distortions induced by interventionist environmental policies or as a natural result of the changing nature of electricity generation. But this is not the case. The market can deliver security. In a competitive market, generators using intermittent sources might have to rely on demand-side mechanisms to balance supply and demand, with their customers facing more volatile prices. Alternatively, they could invest in balancing capacity, or purchase it from the market if necessary. At the same time, energy companies should be allowed to cooperate in order to develop capacity back up and determine how it is financed and supplied to the market when necessary.

For these things to happen, a freer energy market and, at the very least, technology-neutral carbon reduction policies are needed.

PART 5

FROM PLANNING TO MARKET

How is it that these great men have, in their economic writings, been led to make statements about lighthouses that are misleading as to the facts, whose meaning, if thought about in a concrete fashion, is quite unclear, and which, to the extent that they imply a policy conclusion, are very likely wrong?

Ronald H. Coase (1974: 374–75)

14 THE EU 2030 CLIMATE AND ENERGY POLICY FRAMEWORK: ONE STEP FORWARD, ONE STEP BACK

The EU 2030 Framework for Climate and Energy Policy, released in October 2014, seems to partly acknowledge past mistakes, but it fails to make European climate policies consistent with the liberalisation framework that is proposed by electricity directives. However, at least the 2030 framework is more pragmatic and is concerned with containing the monetary costs of environmental targets. This is probably a consequence of the new composition of the European Commission, which – correctly – unifies climate and energy portfolios and emphasises the need to achieve a meaningful 'energy union'.

This energy union is also the subject of a series of communications from the Commission (see, in particular, EC 2015a), which emphasise the need to achieve a greater integration of EU markets. The Energy Union Package recognises that, in order to get to a meaningful single market for energy, national markets should be fully opened. This not only requires the removal of direct interventions in the market, but also necessitates preventing national governments from interfering with markets via other instruments, such as environmental policies and subsidies. Paradoxically, though, the root of such interventionist and distortionary policies is to be found in EU climate directives: Brussels finds itself in a sort of Catch 22. The only way out of this conundrum is to make a clear choice for market liberalisation (Stagnaro 2015).

The new climate framework – which still has to be translated into binding directives by the Commission, after which it will be voted upon by the EU Parliament and eventually introduced by member states in their national legislation – confirms the expected targets, but it seems much more concerned with implementation problems than the previous 2020 package. Moreover, it seems to reflect the awareness that climate policies should be coordinated with, and not at odds with, efforts to open markets. In particular, the framework sets the following targets (EU Council 2014).

- Carbon emissions will be reduced by 40 per cent below 1990 levels: the target will be binding both at the EU level and at the member-state level.

- The EU emissions trading scheme will still be the main policy tool to achieve the decarbonisation target, but several exceptions will be introduced or maintained (including the free allocation of quotas).

- Renewables shall cover at least 27 per cent of total energy consumption at the EU level, but there would be no national targets.

- An 'indicative target' of at least 27 per cent higher energy efficiency will be introduced at the EU level.

- A fully functioning and interconnected internal energy market shall be achieved.

Such targets are the consequence of a compromise between political pressures and vested interests that pushed for the adoption of much more ambitious targets, and forces that called for more realism.

In comparison with the 2020 targets (initially set in 2007), two major differences in the context may explain the different degree of ambition. Firstly, in the past decade the EU has promoted a huge decarbonisation effort, which resulted in the large monetary as well as non-monetary costs discussed above. Secondly, the economic crisis that hit the EU falsified the assumption that electricity demand would keep growing indefinitely, and made stronger the argument for cost benefit analysis of carbon reduction policies. Even the most enthusiastic supporters of green subsidies now admit that past incentives were too high (see, for example, Re Rebaudengo 2014).

Good news and bad news from the 2030 package

This package has been defined as 'a great compromise' (van Renssen 2014): it contains both good news and bad news, though the final outcome will depend on the next steps to be taken by the Commission and the EU Parliament.

The good news is that the new plan, even though it confirms the EU's commitment to act unilaterally on carbon emissions, is more pragmatic than the 2020 package. It seems to be concerned with containing the costs, and it puts more emphasis on the environmental goal of cutting emissions than on the industrial goal of promoting renewables as a particular mechanism of cutting emissions. This is at least partly consistent with the criteria of technological neutrality and market integration, and it should lead to reductions in emissions in the most efficient way possible.

The bad news is that the carbon-reduction goal still seems too ambitious. Or, alternatively, it seems as if the carbon-reduction goal will only be met if there are very low economic growth rates. Moreover, even though an EU-wide renewable energy target is less problematic than 28 national targets, it still suggests that Brussels is pursuing an industrial policy as well as an environmental policy. In other words, Brussels not only cares about the extent of carbon emissions, but also cares about the promotion of renewables as an independent goal. This is at odds with a liberalised market.

Why did the emissions trading system 'fail'?

Much will depend on another legislative move that is going to be a significant part of the deal: the reform of the EU's Emissions

Trading Scheme (ETS) (Buchan et al. 2014). There is little doubt that the ETS underperformed and that it can be much improved (Cló and Vendramin 2012). There is also little doubt that the most recent interventions exacerbated, rather than solved, the short-comings of the ETS (Stagnaro 2013).

EU leaders and green pressure groups criticised the ETS for pricing carbon emissions at a level that was too low, there-fore providing too little incentive for new investments in clean technologies. However, there are two flaws in this reasoning. Firstly, the ETS priced carbon emissions at a low level because EU emissions were already declining despite the scheme. Given the expected emission trends and the emissions cap, the price of allowances was, in fact, the 'right' price insofar as it reflected the marginal cost of carbon abatement given the total cap that was implemented. Secondly, the outcome of a cap-and-trade scheme is not necessarily the promotion of clean fuels: it is the efficient pricing of carbon emissions. Once carbon is priced, businesses and consumers will make their own choices from a wide spec-trum of ways to reduce carbon emissions. This will include, but not be limited to, the following: investing in clean technologies (such as solar or wind power), switching from less clean fuels (such as coal) to cleaner ones (such as natural gas), investing in energy efficiency or paying more for 'dirty' energy if the price of cleaner alternatives is still uncompetitive, even after the social cost of carbon (as reflected by ETS allowances) has been included. An ETS will also help ensure that those who can cut carbon emis-sions most cheaply will do so first.

Challenges for emissions trading system reform

If the ETS reform is aimed at streamlining the system while re-moving the existing distortions (for example, the discretionary distribution of free allowances), then the system will work well. If, instead, the aim of reform is to manipulate the cap-and-trade scheme in order to price carbon in an arbitrary way, then the ETS would lose its potential benefit as an efficient market mechanism for reducing carbon emissions.

If political manipulation of the ETS is not reduced, renewable targets remain binding and capacity support schemes become even more pervasive, then the liberalisation agenda would not be sustainable. Market integration and the so-called energy union would fall apart too. This can be seen quite clearly from the European Commission's own evaluations. The most recent communication on progress towards completing the internal energy market (EC 2014b and EC 2014c), while acknowledging some progress, mentions several concerns.

In particular, the Commission recognises that major challenges lie ahead with regard to 'ensuring the integration of renewables in a secure and reliable manner'. As the Commission itself puts it:

> As renewable penetration increases, it also raises challenges. The variability and limited predictability of solar and wind power make it more demanding to stabilise the grid. Well integrated markets are without any doubt best suited to address that challenge. They make it possible to connect areas with complementary energy mixes and hence make the energy system more resilient to swings in demand or supply.

Unfortunately, as has been detailed, several member states are responding to the instability problems as well as to the financial difficulties of conventional generators by introducing capacity mechanisms. The Commission argues that:

> Whereas well designed measures can offer a proportionate and effective solution to real generation adequacy shortcomings, badly designed schemes will unnecessarily burden consumer bills and may undermine investments in energy efficiency and

new interconnectors and [have an] impact [on] our decarbonisation policy.

But it also warns that 'a regional capacity mechanism within a single price zone would distort market functioning'. The only way to achieve the energy union is by adopting policies that limit the discretionary powers of national governments as well as those of the European Commission. For example, member states must be prevented from introducing policy tools that jeopardise competition. The Commission seems to have understood this, but it does not seem willing to follow such a line. As a result, the 2030 framework, as it has been devised so far, appears to be 'too little, too late', both from the point of view of climate interventionists and from the perspective of those who are more concerned with the internal consistency of competition and environmental policy. In the next chapter, we propose an alternative way forward.

15 THE WAY FORWARD: LAISSEZ-FAIRE

Cutting carbon emissions the expensive way

If the proposal to reduce carbon emissions is accepted, this can be done in ways that distort markets much less than the current approach. In other words, carbon emissions can be reduced to the same extent as current targets but at less cost. Alternatively, for the same cost carbon emissions can be reduced by more than we otherwise could. How can this be done? As has been implied in much of the discussion above, technology-neutral mechanisms such as carbon taxes or emissions trading schemes are likely to achieve the greatest level of carbon reduction for a given cost.

In terms of the objective of promoting carbon reduction for the least cost, the inappropriateness of current policy can easily be described. If a carbon tax had been imposed (or if the only intervention had been a cap-and-trade system), a consumer, see-ing the estimate of the social cost of consuming electricity and emitting carbon as indicated by the carbon tax, would choose the most efficient way to reduce carbon emissions. This might be done by using heating more economically, or by insulating their home to a greater degree. If the tax were imposed uniformly across other activities that involve the emission of carbon (e.g. driving), other possibilities would be available (such as taking fewer car journeys or relying on apps such as Uber rather than using a private car).

If the EU adopts a cap-and-trade policy, the total level of car-bon emissions from electricity production and other relevant activities will, in effect, be capped. Carbon-intensive electricity will become more expensive, as permits to emit carbon will have to be bought. This would have the same effect as a tax. If the EU then subsidises the production of renewables as well, the effect of this will simply be to reduce the price of permits to emit carbon. The price will fall until all the permits to emit carbon have been bought and the capped level of carbon emitted. Even if there were cheaper ways to reduce carbon emissions than producing electricity using renewables, it is simply impossible for such ways to be found and followed. Every extra MWh of electricity produced using renewables might be thought to reduce carbon-intensive production. However, it just leads to a lower price for permits to emit carbon. These permits will be bought and the capped amount of carbon will be released anyway. As has already been discussed, a further cost of cutting carbon emissions in this way is that it injects a large amount of intermittent generation into power systems – a negative externality in itself.

The tension between the decentralised decisions made in a broadly liberalised market and centralised decisions made in the name of environmental policy surfaced when the economic crisis hit Europe. Because of other regulations giving green producers priority access to the market, the fall in demand disproportionately hit conventional generators that were displaced by the subsidised green producers. The challenges of intermittency and the rent-seeking activities of conventional generators led to the widespread adoption of capacity support schemes, which further moved the pendulum towards greater centralisation.

By taking this approach, European policymakers neglected several lessons from economic theory, particularly those related to government failures. Typical examples of government failures are regulatory capture (Stigler 1971; Laffont and Tirole 1991), the crowding out of private investments (Blanchard 2008) and the failure to promote economic growth (Krueger 1990). All of these problems have blighted the EU.

Thus, the first step towards a liberalised electricity market is to move to a technology neutral and economically efficient way of reducing carbon emissions.

Cutting greenhouse gases efficiently

When looking at negative externalities – such as man-made climate change – one should resist the temptation to focus on the short run. In the past 20 years, several environmental economists have found examples of the so-called environmental Kuznets curve: i.e. they have observed that pollutant emissions quite often follow an inverted U-shape curve, whereby they initially increase over time (or with per capita income) but then, as they approach a given level, they tend to turn downwards. There is much discussion about the extent to which the environmental Kuznets curve may be generalised, and whether it is a 'natural phenomenon' or depends on exogenous inputs that may themselves vary with income (see Simon 1996; Grossman and Krueger 1995, 1996; Schmalensee et al. 1998; Goklany 2007; Carson 2010). This may include environmental policies. For example, it may be the case that policy interventions in richer countries lead to a reduction in emissions and, therefore, the Kuznets curve should not itself be used as the only argument against government intervention.

Nevertheless, in the long run, we may well observe two phenomena that will affect the environmental impact of electricity generation, especially in relation to carbon emissions. Cleaner generating technologies will become cheaper. In addition, electricity as a share of total energy consumption will probably grow. Electricity, on average, is both cleaner and easier to control than other forms of energy. So, there may be a natural dynamic towards a more environmentally friendly energy sector. If this is true, we must be very careful that the environmental policies we adopt do not slow down or stifle this natural process by distorting decision-making and preventing the adoption of the most promising and cost-effective innovations. Such innovations may be at the producer level (the production of green energy) or at the consumer level (for example, new methods of reducing energy consumption).

Unfortunately, the EU directives on renewables do seem to have the effect of impeding innovation, though the limited liberalisation of the market that has happened might help counter this. It is crucial that the dynamic efficiency of the market is maximised. This means maximising the effectiveness of the market in gathering dispersed information about the costs and benefits of different approaches to generation and green energy production. In this respect, it is not true – to paraphrase Klein (2015) – that climate change 'changes everything'. While it may be true that climate change poses a serious policy challenge, there are tools to address it, and the tools that will address it most effectively involve using market mechanisms. It is non-market mechanisms that will compromise the extraordinary progress and efficiency gains that have been made possible by well-functioning markets. Indeed, it was nationalisation in the twentieth century that led entire power systems (such as the British one) to be overdependent on domestic coal. This dependence on coal has been unwound in the UK because of privatisation. In the twenty-first century, it may be liberalisation that reconciles the benefits of the electrification of societies with environmental protection.

Lack of competition and the presence of regulatory obstacles stifle the market, crowd out investment, create moral hazard, induce perverse behaviours and provide firms with the ability to exercise market power that they would not have in the absence of environmental regulation.

However, there are major drivers of sustainability built in to market forces in a truly liberalised power market where entry is free and the market is contestable. It is crucial that these positive forces are preserved.

Innovation

The first of these forces is innovation. When it comes to electricity markets, innovation should be embraced in its broadest sense: in generation technologies, network engineering, the development of more efficient energy-consuming devices, the market behaviour of both suppliers and consumers, commercial innovation, marketing and institutional innovation.

A competitive environment creates the conditions in which innovation is maximised. Innovation is more likely to happen within a competitive environment, because suppliers must discover new ways to encourage customers to buy their services and provide these services at a lower cost. Firms also have to find ways to differentiate their products from those of other producers. This challenge is particularly important in the power sector, which has been characterised by a relatively low level of innovation in the past few decades, during which state monopolies dominated the industry.

Lester and Hart (2012) emphasise the importance of '[e]xpanding the domain of market competition, promoting an open industry architecture, and encouraging the entry of new competitors into newly-opened segments of the electric power industry'. Innovation can be very much associated with the achievement of environmental goals. If incentives exist as a result of carbon taxes or cap-and-trade schemes, or simply because consumers value green energy, an open, competitive market will promote innovation to reduce carbon emissions. Indeed, in the past few decades carbon intensity (the ratio of carbon emissions to GDP) has been steadily declining, both at the global and the EU level. There were many drivers underpinning this trend, of course, but increased competition in the energy sector and technological improvements are definitely among the most important ones, especially in transition countries (Cornillie and Fankhauser 2002; Zhang 2013).

To the extent that renewable subsidies undermine open and competitive markets, they can stifle innovation. A report from the International Energy Agency (IEA 2013), which outlines the most promising technological and policy paths for decreasing carbon emissions in the long run, pays relatively little attention to green sources of energy. Instead, it emphasises the role of energy efficiency (this presupposes an active demand side as far as the power markets are concerned), limiting the construction of the least efficient coal-fired plants (but not limiting coal per se), minimising methane emissions from the oil and gas upstream sector and accelerating the phasing out of subsidies to fossil-fuel combustion. The latter measure is, of course, the most consistent with a liberalisation framework, as subsidies distort capital allocation and investment as well as production and consumption patterns. But, more generally, renewable subsidies prevent the market from developing innovations that help to reduce carbon emissions as efficiently as possible – whether they be demand-side or supply-side innovations.

In brief, competition spurs innovation and monopoly and regulation usually do not. To the extent that we believe that innovation is important in reducing carbon emissions, we should be very careful before we forfeit the potential benefits of increased competition.

Efficiency

A second way for liberalisation to reduce environmental impacts is through increased efficiency in production. Even in a market dominated by fossil fuels, such increased efficiency can substantially reduce carbon emissions, as more energy is produced from given inputs. Because inputs are costly to power generators, they have an interest in minimising the level of inputs per unit of energy they produce. But such incentives are absent without functioning markets. Liberalisation is associated with greater efficiency not only in plant use but also in choosing which plant should be employed. Efficiency increases as the market expands. Investments in the power grid are crucial both in terms of increasing competition and ensuring the efficient usage of existing plants (as well as efficient investment in future capacity). But, insofar as markets are balkanised, there will be insufficient interconnection between different centres of production. Keeping the European market segmented is inefficient in that it prevents the efficiencies that can arise from returns to scale, yet it allows national governments to prevent the entry of competitors who might endanger their 'national champions'.

There has been some progress here. National champions still exist, but they have often diversified into other countries so that there is more competition. As a result, there has been growing concentration in the market at the EU level, whilst at the same time more competition at the national level (Jamasb and Pollitt 2005). Nevertheless, there is still much work to do before a truly integrated EU market for electricity is operational. Overall, the integration and liberalisation of European power networks could be an effective environmental policy.

Liberalisation

Electricity liberalisation led to much more careful selection of technologies and investments. Before competition was introduced, the paramount concern of vertically integrated monopolies was to reconcile demand and consumption patterns with their own forecasts, which led to rigid generation fleets characterised by high fixed costs that could be recovered by passing the costs onto consumers through regulated tariffs. After liberalisation, utilities had a strong incentive not only to build efficient units, but also to create efficient fleets. In practice, this meant that the share of high-emissions sources, such as coal, decreased, while large investments were made in cleaner technologies, such as the combined cycle gas turbine (CCGT).

Interestingly enough, the greatest reduction in carbon emissions per unit of power generated in European history did not come from subsidised sources of energy or as a result of regulation, but from businesses following the profit motive in the face of the risk-return profile of different methods of generation. The 'dash for gas' in the UK exemplifies this phenomenon. The new environment created by privatisation and liberalisation of both the electricity and the natural gas industries spurred new investment in upstream natural gas as well as in new electricity generating capacity. Under the new regime, British utilities switched from technologies characterised by high sunk costs – such as nuclear and coal – to natural-gas-fuelled plants (Helm 2003; Pearson and Watson 2012). As a result, UK energy-related greenhouse gas emissions fell from 601.8 million tonnes of CO_2 e[1] in 1990 to 560.3 million tonnes of CO_2 e in 2000 (a fall of nearly 7 per cent), and then to 528.9 million tonnes of CO_2 e in 2010 (a total fall of 12 per cent). While the most recent reductions may be due to the economic downturn, that was not the case in the 1990s. In fact, over the last decade of the twentieth century, real GDP in Britain grew by 37 per cent. Overall, the economy's carbon intensity – i.e. the amount of emissions per unit of GDP – dropped from 0.395 tonnes of CO_2 e per US$1,000 in 1990 to 0.283 tonnes of CO_2 e per US$1,000 in 2000 (a fall of nearly 30 per cent) to 0.227 tonnes of CO_2 e per US$1,000 in 2010 (a total fall of 45 per cent).[2]

The potential role of natural gas in reducing emissions by displacing coal from power production is confirmed by the shale

---

1   Equivalent CO_2 (CO_2 e) is the amount of CO_2 that would cause the same level of radiative forcing as a given amount of greenhouse gases, such as methane, nitrous oxide, etc.

2   The source for this data is the US Energy Information Administration.

Figure 14 Energy-related CO_2 emissions per capita and CO_2 intensity in selected regions

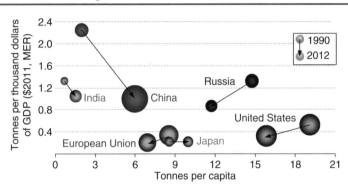

Note: bubbles area indicates total annual energy-related CO_2 emissions in that region. MER denotes market exchange rate.
Source: IEA (2013).

gas revolution in the US. Shale gas has allowed the US to reduce emissions faster than the EU, despite the better economic performance of the former (see Figure 14).

Both the US and the EU have had a significant reduction in both carbon intensity and per capita carbon emissions. In both cases, the recession played a role, although that was more important in the case of Europe, as did the reduction in energy-intensive industries as manufacturing migrated to other countries. But there are also key differences.

The EU spent a huge amount of money promoting renewables. The US instead relied relatively more on market-driven moves to natural gas. Ironically, the more abundant supply of natural gas in the US unlocked huge amounts of coal that were no longer required in the North American market. The EU has a much less open natural gas market (Beccarello and Piron 2008), which is still strongly influenced by national champions, vertically integrated suppliers and politically driven long-term, take-or-pay contracts with foreign suppliers, such as Russia and Algeria (Furfari 2012). As a result, natural gas prices did not experience the same reduction they did in the US, and the cheap US coal actually displaced natural gas to some extent. For example, in 2014 the price of natural gas in the US was about half the level of that in Europe (BP 2015). Coal prices in Europe declined by 32 per cent in 2011–13, leading to higher utilisation rates of existing coal-fuelled power stations. Coal use still declined, under pressure from demand reduction and increasing green generation, but it did not suffer to the extent that natural gas did from such tendencies (Cornot-Gandolphe 2014).

This lesson should be understood by the EU as they design policies that are intended to reduce carbon emissions. Even if policymakers believe they cannot rely on free markets to correctly price negative externalities, including climate change, they should devise policies that supplement markets in internalising the environmental costs of energy production and consumption patterns. But this should be combined with liberalisation and the promotion of competition and innovation.

To give one example, if we ignore geological difficulties, fracking is much harder to exploit in the EU (including the UK) than it is in the US. This is because of a hostile policy environment towards non-renewables, as well as other factors such as population density. More generally, the EU needs to ensure that companies can innovate in order to increase the efficiency of their energy production and move to less carbon-intensive sources of energy.

This is often made more difficult by regulation and the discrimination against all sources of energy that emit carbon (such as natural gas), even if they are relatively cleaner than existing technologies. The US approach – which has delivered cheaper energy and better environmental outcomes – is radically different to the EU approach of picking winners.

Summary

A liberalised energy market and efficient ways of reducing carbon emissions are not objectives that should be in conflict. Indeed, it is impossible to have liberalised energy markets unless carbon reduction policies work with, rather than against, the grain of the market. If carbon reduction policies work against market forces, then the other advantages of a liberalised market are lost too.

The first prerequisite of policy change is to opt for a technology-neutral approach to reducing carbon emissions. Innovation in efficient ways to reduce carbon emissions will naturally follow from that. The second is that competition needs to be promoted. This should include promoting cross-border competition whilst also removing government controls that prevent new and more localised approaches to generating electricity from developing. Finally, there should be a general climate of liberalisation around all aspects of the industry. Experience has shown in both the UK and the US that liberalisation can lead to huge benefits from unexpected sources. For example, the move to gas in the UK in the 1990s and in the US in recent years was facilitated by the liberalisation of the electricity, coal and gas industries in the UK and by the liberal environment surrounding fracked natural gas in the US. In both cases, there were huge benefits, both in terms of reducing the cost of energy and in terms of reducing carbon emissions. These achievements have not been replicated in less liberal environments.

16 CONCLUSION

From state control to liberalisation in the UK

In the post-war period, the electricity industry has been characterised by a significant degree of state control. In some countries, this involved the complete control of every aspect of generation and distribution. This was partly because of the way technology developed. The main technologies created the possibility of natural monopolies, though such natural monopolies did not necessarily pervade all parts of the electricity production process. Furthermore, the intellectual climate in the post-war period favoured using nationalisation and state control to deal with these problems. There were few exceptions to this approach.

However, in the 1980s, things began to change. The UK energy market liberalisation process was the first of its kind in the EU.[1] The process involved defining the natural monopoly more precisely and regulating that part of the system whilst encouraging competition in other aspects of the generation and distribution system. In the UK, that liberalisation came under fire after 2008, partly as a result of the adoption of the particular carbon emission reduction policies that were chosen and which were not compatible with a liberalised market. These policies involved the rejection of an institutional arrangement whereby competitive markets would determine the most efficient way to reduce

---

1   Norway also pioneered electricity liberalisation: see Von der Fehr and Hansen (2010).

carbon emissions. Various regulatory actions were taken in the post-2008 period that reduced competition. In addition, prices started to rise because of the commodity price boom, and this put a very sharp focus on the industry in public debate. In fact, the period of liberalisation before 2008 worked. In particular, it was effective in improving efficiency and reducing prices as well as promoting product differentiation, which were favourable to consumers. Liberalisation also decreased investment and operating costs in the industry and spurred an impressive wave of investment in new generating capacity. Finally, liberalisation contributed (together with other, exogenous factors) to changing the technological paradigm by promoting the gas turbine plants that are now crucial in every power system in Europe. In the UK, from 1990 to 1999, electricity charges for domestic consumers fell by 26 per cent in real terms, with a larger fall for industrial users. It cannot be argued that this was only due to the falling prices of energy commodities in world markets. The whole point is that, until privatisation, electricity companies had to use expensive domestic fuels.

Attempts at liberalisation in the EU

The EU has also tried to promote liberalisation. It has implemented three packages of directives and regulations aimed at progressively opening national electricity markets and promoting their integration. These packages have been relatively successful in meeting their own stated objectives. For example, there is more energy trading between states and more cross border penetration. The average market share of incumbent dominant firms in the EU fell from 64.9 per cent in 1999 to 55.9 per cent in 2010. Private and foreign companies have entered markets that had previously been treated as inherently monopolistic, and that had been dominated by state-owned companies. However, overall, these reforms have not created the paradigm shift in the EU that happened in the UK in the 1990s and early 2000s. The reversal of the trend towards liberalisation in Britain makes it more unlikely than ever that policy will change in the EU.

Misconceived climate policies

The real threat to the liberalisation of the EU electricity industry has come from climate change policy. It is this, together with concerns about energy security, that also led to a reversal of liberalisation in the UK. However, energy security can be entrusted to the market. There tends to be a natural diversity of supply when energy is provided through a decentralised market and suppliers have an incentive to maintain supply. Certainly in the UK, the experience of the state controlling energy was one of serious insecurity over supply problems with an over-reliance on domestically produced coal.

Climate change policies also do not justify an interventionist approach in energy markets. Such policies can be pursued in ways that are technology neutral and preserve the role of markets in making decisions as to how to reduce carbon emissions. Unfortunately, the UK government as well as the EU have moved in the other direction. As Pollitt (2008b) puts it, 'with regard to the balance of liberalisation and regulation in electricity systems, climate change is a potential vehicle for the return of old-style intervention in electricity generation and in retail competition'.

The EU is relying on two major approaches to achieve carbon reduction. The first is an emissions trading system (ETS). Under such a scheme, emission cuts come as a result of independent economic actions that are coordinated by the price system. The cheapest ways of reducing carbon emissions will then tend to be found, which might involve people making decisions to reduce emissions outside the electricity market, or taking action to reduce their consumption. The ETS is not a perfect solution, and better alternatives may exist (for example, a carbon tax). Yet, the

ETS, for all its flaws, is a policy instrument that is consistent with its goal.

The second tool is direct subsidies to renewable energy, with the implementation of this being left to the member states. Renewable subsidies have several inherent faults. Firstly, such subsidies are ultimately discretionary. Secondly, they do not constitute a policy directly aimed at cutting emissions (i.e. at achieving an environmental goal); they are a policy aimed at increasing the production of renewables – other policies are then needed to try to cut emissions. Thirdly, they aim to pick winners, both in relation to trying to select the 'best' form of renewable energy and also in relation to explicitly choosing the increased production of renewables as a mechanism for attempting to reduce carbon emissions. Indeed, given the existence of the ETS, renewables subsidies cannot cut carbon emissions – they can only reduce the price of carbon emissions by reducing the demand for carbon-intensive energy, so that more carbon emissions will be produced elsewhere. The carbon credits that are issued will be bought by somebody.

There are several harmful effects of this policy tool. The costs are substantial – expensive ways of reducing emissions are chosen as a matter of policy. They substantially reduce the quality of electricity provision by creating intermittency. They also undermine competition by narrowing down the part of the market that is truly open to competition. This effect was magnified by the fall in power demand after the financial crisis and subsequent recession.

This leads to further, negative consequences. For a start, the public's support for liberalisation is reduced: if there are no visible benefits, why should the public vote for pro-liberalisation policies? Also, there are several interest groups that have a stake in public policy, and they have an incentive to lobby for favourable treatment. This includes energy-intensive consumers who have asked for (and often obtained) discounted prices paid for by politically weaker residential consumers or SMEs; renewables generators who wish to lobby for subsidies and other special treatments; and conventional generators, who lobby to be paid for providing stand-by spare capacity. Thus, the consequence of the EU and UK approach to emission reductions is that decisions are determined within the political sphere, rather than within the market. One effect of this is more expensive energy with a reduced security of supply. Another effect is that, for any given cost, there will be a smaller reduction in carbon emissions. A further effect is the redistribution of costs onto dispersed consumers and benefits towards more powerful lobby groups.

To sum up, subsidies and regulation create distortions in the market that change behaviour and result in opportunistic actions and a more inherently oligopolistic market structure. These distortions beget more regulation, in part because there is a need to regulate the provision of subsidies, but also because the competitive part of the market is reduced. The very design of the market may be radically changed. The UK's Electricity Market Reform, which stifles competition both in the wholesale and retail electricity markets, provides a good example of this. This book has been much more concerned with market design than market structure, but subsidies, by altering that design, also change the structure.

Fundamental misunderstandings

The whole problem, beyond its rent-seeking and ideological dimensions, derives from a deep misunderstanding of Hayek's lesson about competition and markets. Both the use of green subsidies and the subsequent regulatory adjustments, such as capacity mechanisms, rely on the idea that the regulators know what they, in fact, do not know. This 'knowledge problem' relates to issues such as the optimum level of CO_2 emissions, the most efficient ways to reduce emissions and the level of spare capacity it is necessary for the market to hold. The answers to these questions can only be discovered in a liberalised and decentralised competitive market. Despite the public emphasis on competition, the environmental takeover of European energy policies is effectively recentralising the decision-making process that had been decentralised to some extent.

The 'knowledge problem' should be taken seriously, especially by environmentalists, given the importance they attach to their goals. An environmental goal can be achieved by setting the goal itself and relying on human and entrepreneurial ingenuity to find ways to get the hoped-for result. Thus, liberalisation can provide answers to environmental problems, and environmental policies can be devised that are consistent with a liberalised framework. Alternatively, we can centrally plan our way to reducing emissions, an approach that will not succeed without huge costs.

The EU has released a new decarbonisation plan that, in part, seems to acknowledge past mistakes, but it does too little to reverse the trend. The regulatory measures taken in several EU member states, either driven by or on top of EU directives, show that the temptation to command and control is much stronger than the belief in competition for most policymakers. It is ironic that the UK, which once led the way in terms of promoting market opening reforms, is now at the forefront of the counter-reformers.

REFERENCES

Abrell, J. and Weigt, H. (2008) The interaction of emissions trading and renewable energy promotion. Dresden University of Technology Working Paper WP-EGW-05.

ACER (2014) Annual report on the results of monitoring the internal electricity and natural gas markets in 2013. ACER, Ljubljana, SI.

Alchian, A. (1950) Uncertainty, evolution, and economic theory. *Journal of Political Economy* 58(3): 211–21.

Allen & Overy (2012) UK electricity market reform: the energy bill overview. December 2012.

Amundsen, E. S., Bergman, L. and Von Der Fehr, N.-H. M. (2006) The Nordic electricity market: robust by design? In *Electricity Market Reform: An International Perspective* (ed. F. Sioshansi and W. Pfaffenberger), pp. 145–70. Amsterdam: Elsevier.

Anderson, T. L. and Leal, D. R. (2001) [1991] *Free Market Environmentalism*. London, UK: Palgrave MacMillan.

Ausubel, L. M. and Cramton, P. (2010) Using forward markets to improve electricity market design. *Utilities Policy* 18(2): 195–200.

Bartle, I. (ed.) (2003) The UK model of utility regulation. A 20th anniversary collection to mark the 'Littlechild Report' retrospect and prospect. Proceedings of a Joint LBS Regulation Initiative, CRI and City University Business School Conference, CBI Proceedings 31.

Bastiat, F. (1998) [1850] *The Law*. Irvington-on-Hudson, NY: Foundation for Economic Education.

Batlle, C. and Rodilla, P. (2010) A critical assessment of the different approaches aimed to secure electricity generation supply. *Energy Policy* 38(11): 7169–79.

Baumol, W. T. (1977) On the proper cost tests for natural monopoly in a multiproduct industry. *American Economic Review* 67(5): 809–22.

Baumol, W. T. (1982) Contestable markets: an uprising in the theory of industry structure. *American Economic Review* 72(1): 1–15.

Beccarello, M. and Piron, F. (2008) La regolazione del mercato del gas naturale. Rubbettino, Soveria Mannelli, CZ, IT.

Beckman, K. (2011) Our unpredictable, bright energy future. *European Energy Review*, 7 April.

Beckman, K. (2014) Brussels concludes UK measures for Hinkley Point nuclear power plant are compatible with EU rules. *EnergyPost.eu*, 8 October.

Beesley, M. and Littlechild, S. C. (1983) Privatisation: principles, problems and priorities. *Lloyd Banks Review* 149: 1–20.

Beesley, M. and Littlechild, S. C. (1989) The regulation of privatized monopolies in the United Kingdom. *Rand Journal of Economics* 20(3): 454–72.

Benedettini, S. (2014a) Mercato elettrico. In *Indice delle liberalizzazioni 2014* (ed. C. Stagnaro), pp. 57–64. Torino: IBL Libri.

Benedettini, S. (2014b) Capacity market UK: buon design ma il problema è nel manico. Staffetta Quotidiana, 23 December.

Benedettini, S. (2015) Electricity and natural gas market. In *Index of Liberalization 2015* (ed. C. Stagnaro). Torino: IBL Libri.

Benedettini, S. and Stagnaro, C. (2014) The case for allowing negative electricity prices. *EnergyPost.eu*, 27 May.

Benedettini, S. and Stagnaro, C. (2015) Failure to liberalise energy retail markets jeopardises energy union. *EnergyPost.eu*, 16 January.

Blanchard, O. J. (2008) Crowding out. In *The New Palgrave Dictionary of Economics* (ed. S. N. Durlauf and L. E. Blume). Basingstoke, UK: Palgrave Macmillan.

Bodanis, D. (2005) *Electric Universe: The Shocking True Story of Electricity*. New York City: Crown.

Boffa, F., Pingali, V. and Vannoni, D. (2010) Increasing market interconnection: an analysis of the Italian electricity spot market. *International Journal of Industrial Organization* 28(3): 311–22.

Borenstein, S. (2011) The private and public economics of renewable electricity generation. The National Bureau of Economic Research, NBER Working Paper 17695.

Borenstein, S. and Bushnell, J. (2000) Electricity restructuring: deregulation or regulation. *Regulation* 23(2): 46–52.

Bortolotti, B., Cambini, C., Rondi, L. and Spiegel, Y. (2011) Capital structure and regulation: do ownership and regulatory independence matter? *Journal of Economics & Management Strategies* 20(2): 517–64.

BP (2015) *Statistical Review of World Energy 2015*.

Braathen, N. A. (2011) Interactions between emission trading systems and other overlapping policy instruments. OECD Green Growth Papers 2011-02.

Bradley Jr, R. L. (2004) *Climate Alarmism Reconsidered*. London: Institute of Economic Affairs.

Braun, J. F. (2011) EU energy policy under the Treaty of Lisbon rules: between a new policy and business as usual. EPIN Working Paper 31.

Bronson, R. and Levy, P. (2014) How much is the US–China deal worth? *Foreign Policy*, 14 November.

Bryce, R. (2009) *Gusher of Lies: The Dangerous Delusions of 'Energy Independence'*. New York: PublicAffairs.

Buchan, D., Keay, M. and Robinson, D. (2014) Energy and climate targets for 2030: Europe takes its foot off the pedal. The Oxford Institute for Energy Studies, Oxford Energy Comment, October 2014.

Burrell, A. (ed.) (2010) Impacts of the EU biofuel target on agricultural markets and land use: a comparative modelling assessment. European Commission Joint Research Center and Institute for Prospective Technical Studies, JRC Scientific and Technical Reports, EUR 24449 EN.

Carlton, D. W. and Peltzman, S. (2010) Introduction to Stigler's theory of oligopoly. *Competition Policy International* 6(2): 237–51.

Carson, R. T. (2010) The environmental Kuznets curve: seeking empirical regularity and theoretical structure. *Review of Environmental Economics and Policy* 4(1): 3–23.

CEER (2013) Status review of renewable and energy efficiency support schemes in Europe. C12-SDE-33-03.

Chapman, S. J. (2002) *Electric Machinery and Power System Fundamentals*. Columbus, OH: McGraw-Hill.

Clò, A. (2008) *Il Rebus Energetico*. Bologna, Italy: Il Mulino.

Clò, S. and Vendramin, E. (2012) Is the ETS still the best option? *Istituto Bruno Leoni*, Special Report, 10 May.

CMA (2015a) Energy market investigation. Provisional findings report, 7 July.

CMA (2015b) Energy market investigation. Notice of possible remedies, 7 July.

Coase, R. H. (1937) The nature of the firm. *Economica* 4(16): 386–405.

Coase, R. H. (1960) The problem of social cost. *Journal of Law and Economics* 3(1): 1–44.

Coase, R. H. (1974) The lighthouse in economics. *Journal of Law and Economics* 17(2): 357–76.

Cochrane, J. H. (2015) Carbon tax or carbon rights? *The Grumpy Economist Blog*, 5 January.

Considine, T. J. and Kleit, A. N. (2007) Can electricity restructuring survive? Lessons from California and Pennsylvania. In *Electric Choices* (ed. A. N. Kleit), pp. 9–38. Lanham, MD: Rowman & Littlefield.

Conway, P. and Nicoletti, G. (2006) Product market regulation in non-manufacturing sectors in OECD countries: measurement and highlights. OECD Economics Department, Working Paper 530.

Cornillie, J. and Fankhauser, S. (2002) The energy intensity of transition countries. European Bank for Reconstruction and Development Working Paper 72.

Cornot-Gandolphe, S. (2014) *Gas and Coal Competition in the EU Power Sector*. Rueil Malmaison, France: Cedigaz.

Couture, T. D., Cory, K., Kreycik, C. and Williams, E. (2010) A policymaker's guide to feed-in tariff policy design. NREL Technical Report NREL/TP-6A2-44849.

Cramton, P. and Ockenfelds, A. (2011) Economics and design of capacity markets for the power sector. University of Maryland Working Paper, 30 May.

Cramton, P., Ockenfelds, A. and Stoft, S. (2013) Capacity market fundamentals. *Economics of Energy and Environmental Policy* 2(2): 27–46.

DECC (2012) Electricity market reform: policy overview. May 2012.

DECC (2013) Electricity generation cost 2013. Department of Energy & Climate Change, London, UK.

De Meulemeester, B. (2014) Capacity payments: expensive solution for a non-existing problem. *EnergyPost.eu*, 24 June.

Demsetz, H. (1968) Why regulate utilities? *Journal of Law and Economics* 11(1): 55–66.

De Paoli, L. and Gulli', F. (2010) Bilancio della liberalizzazione del mercato dell'elettricità e del gas in Italia: 1999–2009. *Economics and Policy of Energy and the Environment* 53(2): 5–38.

DOE (2006) Benefits of using mobile transformers and mobile substations for rapidly restoring electric service: a report to the United States Congress pursuant to section 1816 of the Energy Policy Act of 2005. US Department of Energy, Washington, DC.

Drechsler, M., Meyerhoff, J. and Ohl, C. (2012) The effect of feed-in tariffs on the production cost and the landscape externalities of wind power generation in West Saxony, Germany. *Energy Policy* 48(C): 730–36.

EC (2007a) DG competition report on energy sector inquiry. 10 January.

EC (2007b) An energy policy for Europe. COM(2007) 1.

EC (2009) The renewable energy progress report. COM(2009) 192.

EC (2013a) Renewable energy progress report. COM(2013) 175.

EC (2013b) Renewable energy progress report, Commission Staff Working Document. SWD(2013) 102.

EC (2014a) *EU Energy in Figures*. Statistical Pocketbook 2014, Brussels, EU.

EC (2014b) Progress towards completing the internal energy market. COM(2014) 634 final.

EC (2014c) Trends and developments in european energy markets 2014. SWD(2014) 310 final.

EC (2015a) A framework strategy for a resilient energy union with a forward-looking climate change policy. COM(2015) 80 final.

EC (2015b) Delivering a new deal for energy consumers. SWD (2015) 141 final.

EC (2015c) *EU Energy in Figures*. Statistical Pocketbook 2015, Brussels, EU.

ECOFYS (2011) Financing renewable energy in the european energy market. PECPNL084659.

ECOFYS (2014) Subsidies and costs of EU energy. An interim report. Report prepared for the European Commission.

Economist (2013) The cost del sol. *The Economist*, 20 July.

Economist (2014) Sunny, windy, costly and dirty. *The Economist*, 18 January 2014.

Edenhofer, O., Normark, B. and Tardieu, B. (2014) Reform options for the European Emissions Trading Scheme (ETS). Euro-CASE Policy Position Paper, September 2014.

ENTSO-E (2013) Scenario outlook and adequacy forecast 2013–2030.

Epstein, A. (2014) *The Moral Case for Fossil Fuels*. New York: Portfolio/Penguin.

EU Council (2014) Conclusions on the 2030 Climate and Energy Policy Framework, 23–24 October.

Eurelectric (2012) Power statistics & trends 2012.

Eurelectric (2014) Renewable energy and security of supply: finding market solutions. Eurelectric Report, October 2014.

Eurobarometer (2008) Eurobarometer 69, May 2008.

Flint, C. (2014) Speech to the Economist Energy Conference 2014.

Forte, F. (2007) Coase theorem revisited. *Rivista di diritto finanziario e scienza delle finanze* 66(3): 348–63.

Furfari, S. (2012) *Politique et Géopolitique de l'Énergie*. Paris, France: Editions Technip.

Giberson, M. and Kiesling, L. L. (2004) Analyzing the blackout report's recommendations: alternatives for a flexible, dynamic grid. *Energy Policy* 17(6): 51–9.

Glachant, J.-M. (2014) A new energy policy for the new European Commission? *EU Energy Policy Blog*, 4 December.

Glachant, J.-M., Lévêque, F. and Ranci, P. (2008) Some guideposts on the road to formulating a coherent policy on EU energy security of supply. *Electricity Journal* 21(10): 13–18.

Goklany, I. M. (2007) The improving state of the world: why we're living longer, healthier, more comfortable lives on a cleaner planet. Cato Institute, Washington, DC.

Gross, R. (2010) Time to stop experimenting with UK renewable energy policy. ICEPT Working Paper 2010/003.

Grossman, G. M. and Krueger, A. B. (1995) Economic growth and the environment. *Quarterly Journal of Economics* 110(2): 353–77.

Grossman, G. M. and Krueger, A. B. (1996) The inverted U: what does it mean? *Environment and Development Economics* 1(1): 119–22.

Hadjipaschalis, I., Poullikkas, A. and Efthimiou, V. (2009) Overview of current and future energy storage technologies for electric power applications. *Renewable and Sustainable Energy Reviews* 13: 1513–22.

Harker, M. and Waddams-Price, C. (2006) Introducing competition and deregulating the British domestic energy markets: a legal and economic discussion. CCP Working Paper 06-20.

Harris, R. (2001) Can European Union survive? *Economic Affairs* 21(1): 43–6.

Hayek, F. A. (1945) The use of knowledge in society. *American Economic Review* 35(4): 519–30.

Hayek, F. A. (1988) *The Fatal Conceit: The Errors of Socialism*. London: Routledge.

Helm, D. (2003) *Energy, the State, and the Market*. Oxford University Press.

Helm, D. (2009) Climate-change policy: why has so little been achieved? In *The Economics and Politics of Climate Change* (ed. D. Helm and C. Hepburn), pp. 9–35. Oxford University Press.

Helm, D. (2010) Government failure, rent-seeking, and capture: the design of climate change policy. *Oxford Review of Economic Policy* 26(2): 182–96.

Helm, D. (2012) *The Carbon Crunch*. London: Yale University Press.

Henderson, D. (2013) The more things change.... *Nuclear Engineering International*, May 2013.

Henriot, A. and Glachant, J.-M. (2013) Melting-pots and salad bowls: The current debate on electricity market design for integration of intermittent RES. *Utilities Policy* 27(C): 57–64.

Hepburn, C. (2006) Regulation by prices, quantities, or both: a review of instrument choice. *Oxford Review of Economic Policy* 22(2): 259–79.

Hirth, L. (2013) The market value of variable renewables. The effect of solar wind power variability on their relative price. *Energy Economics* 38(C): 218–36.

Hirth, L., Ueckerdt, F. and Edenhofer, O. (2015) Integration costs revisited – an economic framework for wind and solar variability. *Renewable Energy* 74(C): 925–39.

HSBC (2012) Utilities. EMEA Equity Research, July 2012.

IEA (2013) Redrawing the energy-climate map. World Energy Outlook Special Report, 10 June.

IEFE (2013) PJM and ISO-NE forward capacity markets: a critical assessment.

Infantino, L. (2002) *Ignorance and Liberty*. London: Routledge.

IPCC (2007) Climate change 2007. Synthesis Report, Intergovernmental Panel on Climate Change, Geneva, Switzerland.

IPCC (2013) Climate change 2013. The Physical Science Basis, Intergovernmental Panel on Climate Change, Geneva, Switzerland.

Ivaldi, M., Jullien, B., Rey, P., Seabright, P. and Tirole, J. (2003) The economics of tacit collusion. IDEI Report prepared for the European Commission's DG Competition.

Jamasb, T. and Pollitt, M. (2005) Electricity market reform in the European Union: review of progress toward liberalization and integration. *Energy Journal* 26 (Special Issue): 11–42.

Joskow, P. L. (2007) Regulation of natural monopolies. In *Handbook of Law and Economics* (ed. A. M. Polinsky and S. Shavel). Amsterdam: Elsevier Science Publishing.

Joskow, P. L. (2008) Lessons learned from electricity markets liberalization. *Energy Journal*, Special Issue: *The Future of Electricity: Papers in Honor of David Newbery*.

Kiesling, L. L. (2007) The role of retail pricing in electricity restructuring. In *Electric Choices* (ed. A. N. Kleit), pp. 39–62. Lanham, MD: Rowman & Littlefield.

Kiesling, L. L. (2008) *Deregulation, Innovation and Market Liberalization*. London: Routledge.

Kiesling, L. L. (2010) Promoting innovation in the electricity industry. *Economic Affairs* 30(2): 6–12.

Kiesling, L. L. (2015) Power Up. The framework for a new era of UK energy distribution. Report prepared for the Adam Smith Institute.

Kirzner, I. M. (1992) *The Meaning of Market Process*. London: Routledge.

Kirzner, I. M. (1997) Entrepreneurial discovery and the competitive market process: an Austrian approach. *Journal of Economic Literature* 35(1): 60–85.

Klein, N. (2015) *This Changes Everything*. New York: Simon & Schuster.

Kleit, A. N. and Michaels, R. J. (2013) Does competitive electricity require capacity markets? The Texas experience. Texas Public Policy Foundation, February 2013.

Korchinski, W. (2013) The limits of wind power. Reason Foundation Policy Study 403.

Koske, I., Wanner, I., Bitetti, R. and Barbiero, O. (2015) The 2013 update of the OECD product market regulation indicators: policy insights for OECD and non-OECD countries. OECD Economics Department Working Papers 1200/2015.

Krueger, A. O. (1974) The political economy of the rent-seeking society. *American Economic Review* 64(3): 291–303.

Krueger, A. O. (1990) Government failures in development. *Journal of Economic Perspectives* 4(3): 9–23.

Laffont, J.-J. and Tirole, J. (1991) The politics of government decision-making: a theory of regulatory capture. *Quarterly Journal of Economics* 106(4): 1089–127.

Lawson, N. (1982) Speech on energy policy. Speech given at the Fourth Annual International Conference, International Association of Energy Economists, Churchill College, Cambridge, 28 June. Reproduced in 1989 in *The Market for Energy* (D. Helm, J. Kay and D. Thompson). Oxford: Clarendon Press.

Lester, R. K. and Hart, D. M. (2012). *Unlocking Energy Innovation*. Boston, MA: MIT Press.

Littlechild, S. C. (1983) Regulation of British telecommunications' profitability. Department of Industry, London, UK.

Littlechild, S. C. (2000) Privatisation, competition and regulation. IEA Occasional Paper 110.

Littlechild, S. C. (2010) The creation of a market for retail electricity supply. European University Institute Working Paper RSCAS 2010/57.

Littlechild, S. C. (2014) The competition assessment framework for the retail energy sector: some concerns about the proposed interpretation. *European Competition Journal* 10(1): 181–202.

Littlechild, S., McCarthy, C., Marshall, E., Smith, S. and Spottiswoode, C. (2015) Submission on summary of provisional findings and notice of possible remedies. 16 July 2015.

McKenzie, R. B. (ed.) (1984) Plant closings: public or private choices? The Cato Institute, Washington, DC.

Meunier, G. (2010) Capacity choice, technology mix, and market power. *Energy Economics* 32(6): 1306–15.

Mityakov, S. and Portnykh, M. (2012) The infant industry argument and renewable energy production. George C. Marshall Institute, 20 December.

Montgomery, W. D. and Tuladhar, S. D. (2006) Econometric evidence on the relationship between institutional factors and energy intensity. In *The Asia Pacific Partnership: Its Role in Promoting a Positive Climate for Investment, Economic Growth and Greenhouse Gas Reduction* (ed. W. D. Montgomery and S. D. Tuladhar), pp. 35–44. Washington, DC: CRA International and ICCF.

Moran, A. and Skinner, B. (2008) Resource adequacy and efficient infrastructure investment. In *Competitive Electricity Markets. Design, Implementation, Performance* (ed. F. P. Sioshansi), pp. 387–415. Amsterdam: Elsevier.

Moran, M. (2003) *The British Regulatory State.* Oxford University Press.

Myddelton, D. R. (2014) The British approach to privatisation. *Economic Affairs* 34(2): 129–38.

Newbery, D. (2006) Electricity liberalization in Britain and the evolution of market design. In *Electricity Market Reform: An International Perspective* (ed. F. Sioshansi and W. Pfaffenberger), pp. 109–44. Amsterdam: Elsevier.

Newbery, D. and Pollitt, M. (1997) The restructuring and privatization of Britain's CEGB – was it worth it? *Journal of Industrial Economics* 45(3): 269–303.

Nicolazzi, M. (2009) *Il Prezzo Del Petrolio.* Milan, IT: Boroli.

Nordhaus, W. D. (2008) *A Question of Balance. Weighing the Options on Global Warming Policies.* New Haven, CT: Yale University Press.

North, D. C. (1991) Institutions. *Journal of Economic Perspectives* 5(1): 97–112.

Odell, P. R. (2004) *Why Carbon Fuels Will Dominate the 21st Century's Global Energy Economy.* Brentwood, Essex: Multi-Science Publishing.

OECD (2010) Privatisation in the 21st century. Report, January.

OFGEM (2015) Ofgem opens investigations into five generators' compliance with capacity market rules. 21 May.

Parr, M. (2015) UK 'capacity market' is not a market – it's state aid (£1 billion/year). *EnergyPost.eu*, 26 January.

Pearson, P. and Watson, J. (2012) UK energy policy 1980–2010: a history and lessons to be learnt. The Institution of Engineering and Technology – Parliamentary Group for Energy Studies, London, UK.

Peltzman, S. (1975) The effects of automobile safety regulation. *Journal of Political Economy* 83(4): 677–726.

Peltzman, S. (1976) Toward a more general theory of regulation. *Journal of Law and Economics* 19(2): 211–40.

Peltzman, S. (2010) Regulation and the natural progress of opulence. *Economic Affairs* 30(2): 33–9.

Pepermans, G., Driesen, J., Haeseldonckx, D., Belmans, R. and D'Haeseleer, W. (2005) Distributed generation: definition, benefits and issues. *Energy Policy* 33(6): 787–98.

Pfau, R. (1985) *No Sacrifice Too Great: The Life of Lewis L. Strauss*. Charlottesville, VA: University of Virginia Press.

Pickard, J. (2015) Jeremy Corbyn drops plans to nationalise energy groups. *Financial Times*, 29 September.

Pigou, A. C. (1932) [1920] *The Economics of Welfare*. London: Macmillan.

Pollitt, M. G. (2008a) The arguments for and against ownership unbundling of energy transmission networks. *Energy Policy* 36(2): 704–13.

Pollitt, M. G. (2008b) Liberalization and regulation in electricity systems – how can we get the balance right? In *Competitive Electricity Markets. Design, Implementation, Performance* (ed. F. P. Sioshansi), pp. xxii–xxxiv. Amsterdam: Elsevier.

Posner, R. A. (1969) Natural monopoly and regulation. *Stanford Law Review* 21(3): 548–643.

Rassenti, S., Smith, V. L. and Wilson, B. J. (2002) Using experiments to inform the privatization/deregulation movement in electricity. *Cato Journal* 21(3): 515–44.

Reed, S. (2015) Britain plans to cut subsidies for renewable energy. *New York Times*, 22 July 2015.

Re Rebaudengo, A. (2014) Italy's renewable-energy incentive schemes are working. *Wall Street Journal*, 24 September 2014.

Riezner, R. and Testa, F. (2003) The captive consumer no longer exists. Creating customer loyalty to compete on the new deregulated markets of public utilities. *Total Quality Management & Business Excellence* 14(2): 171–87.

Rious, V., Roques, F. and Perez, Y. (2012) Which electricity market design to encourage the development of demand response? European University Institute Working Paper 2012/12.

Robinson, C. (ed.) (2006) The new economics of energy security. Economic Research Council, London, UK.

Robinson, C. (ed.) (2008) *Climate Change Policy: Challenging the Activists*. Institute of Economic Affairs, London, UK.

Robinson, C. (2013) From nationalisation to state control. The return of centralised energy planning. IEA Discussion Paper 49.

Roques, F. (2008) Market design for generation adequacy: healing causes rather than symptoms. *Utilities Policy* 16(3): 171–83.

Sala-i-Martin, X. (2002) 15 years of new growth economics: what have we learnt? Columbia University Department of Economics Discussion Paper 0102-47.

Scarpa, C., Bianchi, P., Bortolotti, B. and Pellizzola, L. (2010) *Comuni S.p.A. Il Capitalismo Municipale in Italia*. Bologna, Italy: Il Mulino.

Schmalensee, R., Stoker, T. M. and Judson, R. A. (1998) World carbon dioxide emissions: 1950–2050. *The Review of Economics and Statistics* 80(1): 15–27.

Schuman, R. (1950) The Schuman Declaration. 9 May.

Seralles, R. J. (2006) Electric energy restructuring in the European Union: integration, subsidiarity and the challenge of harmonization. *Energy Policy* 34(16): 2542–51.

Simon, J. L. (1996) *The Ultimate Resource 2*. Princeton University Press.

Smil, V. (2005) *Creating the Twentieth Century: Technical Innovations of 1867–1914*. Oxford University Press.

Smil, V. (2010) *Energy Transitions: History, Requirements, Prospects*. Santa Barbara, CA: Praeger.

Smil, V. (2014) The long slow rise of solar and wind. *Scientific American* 282(1): 52–7.

Stagnaro, C. (2013) Backloading and credibility of European climate policies. *Energy Tribune*, 5 July.

Stagnaro, C. (2014a) Privatisation in the EU energy sector: the never-ending story. *Economic Affairs* 34(2): 238–53.

Stagnaro, C. (2014b) Italy powers down energy subsidies. *Wall Street Journal*, 2 September.

Stagnaro, C. (2015) The energy union: why liberalisation matters. Epicenter Briefing, 12 March.

Stagnaro, C. and Booth, P. (2015) Consumer inertia in energy markets: a sobering lesson from Italy. *IEA Blog*, 20 July.

Stagnaro, C. and Testa, F. (2011) Reti di trasporto nazionale e concorrenza nei mercati del gas: il caso Eni-Snam Rete Gas. *Sinergie* 86: 187–203.

Stagnaro, C. and Testa, F. (2013) Mercato e regolazione nel settore dell'energia in italia: il caso della delibera Aeeg in tema di materia prima gas. *Management delle Utilities* 3(2013): 64–75.

Stern, J. P. (ed.) (2012) *The Pricing of Internationally Traded Gas*. Oxford: Oxford Institute for Energy Studies.

Stern, J. P. (2014) The British utility regulation model: its recent history and future prospects. CCRP Working Paper 23.

Stigler, G. J. (1971) The theory of economic regulation. *Bell Journal of Economics and Management Science* 2(1): 3–21.

Stigler, G. J. (1974) Free riders and collective action: an appendix to theories of economic regulation. *Bell Journal of Economics and Management Science* 5(2): 359–65.

Stoft, S. (2002) *Power System Economics*. Indianapolis, IN: Wiley Interscience.

Tesla, N. (2013) [1919] *My Inventions: The Autobiography of Nikola Tesla*. London: Soho Books.

Tindale, S. (2015) What the new Conservative government means for UK energy policy. *EnergyPost.eu*, 11 May.

Toledo, O. M., Oliveira Filho, D. and Diniz, A. S. A. C. (2010) Distributed photovoltaic generation and energy storage systems: a review. *Renewable and Sustainable Energy Reviews* 14(1): 506–11.

Van den Bergh, R. J. and Pacces, A. (eds) (2010) *Regulation and Economics. Encyclopedia of Law and Economics*, Vol. 9, 2nd edn. Cheltenham: Edward Elgar.

Van Renssen, S. (2014a) Hinkley Point C: the EU energy market will not be the same after this. *EnergyPost.eu*, 10 October.

Van Renssen, S. (2014b) The EU's great 2030 energy and climate compromise. *EnergyPost.eu*, 24 October.

Van Renssen, S. (2014c) UK capacity market 'will boost baseload not balancing power'. *EnergyPost.eu*, 5 September.

Vasconcelos, J. (2004) Services of general interest and regulation in the EU energy market. Council of European Energy Regulators (CEER) Presentation at XVI CEEP Congress, 17 June, Leipzig.

Verde, S. (2012) Londra 2012. La maratona (a ostacoli) della riforma del settore elettrico britannico. IBL Focus 209.

Von der Fehr, N.-H. M. and Hansen, P. V. (2010) Electricity retailing in Norway. *Energy Journal* 31(1): 25–45.

Weitzman, M. L. (1974) Prices vs. quantities. *Review of Economic Studies* 41(4): 477–91.

Williamson, O. E. (1975) *Markets and Hierarchies*. New York City: Free Press.

Williamson, O. E. (1985) *The Economic Institutions of Capitalism: Firms, Markets, Relational Contracting*. New York City, NY: Free Press.

Yandle, B. (1999) Bootleggers and baptists in retrospect. *Regulation* 22(3): 5–7.

Yandle, B. (2000) Bootleggers, baptists, and global warming. In *The Greening of US Foreign Policy* (ed. T. L. Anderson and H. I. Miller), pp. 195–220. Stanford, CA: The Hoover Institution.

Yarrow, G. (2012) The UK's carbon floor policy. Regulatory Policy Institute Letters & Notes on Regulation 1.2.

Zerbe Jr, R. O. and McCurdy, H. E. (1999) The failure of market failure. *Journal of Policy Analysis and Management* 18(4): 558–78.

Zhang, F. (2013) The energy transition of the transition economies. an empirical analysis. The World Bank Policy Research Working Paper 6387.

Zorzoli, G. B. (2011) *I Due Volti del Mercato Elettrico*. Rome, Italy: AIEE.

ABOUT THE IEA

The Institute is a research and educational charity (No. CC 235 351), limited by guarantee. Its mission is to improve understanding of the fundamental institutions of a free society by analysing and expounding the role of markets in solving economic and social problems.

The IEA achieves its mission by:

- a high-quality publishing programme
- conferences, seminars, lectures and other events
- outreach to school and college students
- brokering media introductions and appearances

The IEA, which was established in 1955 by the late Sir Antony Fisher, is an educational charity, not a political organisation. It is independent of any political party or group and does not carry on activities intended to affect support for any political party or candidate in any election or referendum, or at any other time. It is financed by sales of publications, conference fees and voluntary donations.

In addition to its main series of publications the IEA also publishes a quarterly journal, *Economic Affairs*.

The IEA is aided in its work by a distinguished international Academic Advisory Council and an eminent panel of Honorary Fellows. Together with other academics, they review prospective IEA publications, their comments being passed on anonymously to authors. All IEA papers are therefore subject to the same rigorous independent refereeing process as used by leading academic journals.

IEA publications enjoy widespread classroom use and course adoptions in schools and universities. They are also sold throughout the world and often translated/reprinted.

Since 1974 the IEA has helped to create a worldwide network of 100 similar institutions in over 70 countries. They are all independent but share the IEA's mission.

Views expressed in the IEA's publications are those of the authors, not those of the Institute (which has no corporate view), its Managing Trustees, Academic Advisory Council members or senior staff.

Members of the Institute's Academic Advisory Council, Honorary Fellows, Trustees and Staff are listed on the following page.

The Institute gratefully acknowledges financial support for its publications programme and other work from a generous benefaction by the late Professor Ronald Coase.

A U-Turn on the Road to Serfdom
Grover Norquist
Occasional Paper 150; ISBN 978-0-255-36686-1; £10.00

New Private Monies – A Bit-Part Player?
Kevin Dowd
Hobart Paper 174; ISBN 978-0-255-36694-6; £10.00

From Crisis to Confidence – Macroeconomics after the Crash
Roger Koppl
Hobart Paper 175; ISBN 978-0-255-36693-9; £12.50

Advertising in a Free Society
Ralph Harris and Arthur Seldon
With an introduction by Christopher Snowdon
Hobart Paper 176; ISBN 978-0-255-36696-0; £12.50

Selfishness, Greed and Capitalism: Debunking Myths about the Free Market
Christopher Snowdon
Hobart Paper 177; ISBN 978-0-255-36677-9; £12.50

Waging the War of Ideas
John Blundell
Occasional Paper 131; ISBN 978-0-255-36684-7; £12.50

Brexit: Directions for Britain Outside the EU
Ralph Buckle, Tim Hewish, John C. Hulsman, Iain Mansfield and Robert Oulds
Hobart Paperback 178; ISBN 978-0-255-36681-6; £12.50

Flaws and Ceilings – Price Controls and the Damage They Cause
Edited by Christopher Coyne and Rachel Coyne
Hobart Paperback 179; ISBN 978-0-255-36701-1; £12.50

Scandinavian Unexceptionalism: Culture, Markets and the Failure of Third-Way Socialism
Nima Sanandaji
Readings in Political Economy 1; ISBN 978-0-255-36704-2; £10.00

Classical Liberalism – A Primer
Eamonn Butler
Readings in Political Economy 2; ISBN 978-0-255-36707-3; £10.00

Federal Britain: The Case for Decentralisation
Philip Booth
Readings in Political Economy 3; ISBN 978-0-255-36713-4; £10.00

Forever Contemporary: The Economics of Ronald Coase
Edited by Cento Veljanovski
Readings in Political Economy 4; ISBN 978-0-255-36710-3; £15.00

Other IEA publications

Comprehensive information on other publications and the wider work of the IEA can be found at www.iea.org.uk. To order any publication please see below.

Personal customers

Orders from personal customers should be directed to the IEA:

Clare Rusbridge
IEA
2 Lord North Street
FREEPOST LON10168
London SW1P 3YZ
Tel: 020 7799 8907. Fax: 020 7799 2137
Email: sales@iea.org.uk

Trade customers

All orders from the book trade should be directed to the IEA's distributor:

NBN International (IEA Orders)
Orders Dept.
NBN International
10 Thornbury Road
Plymouth PL6 7PP
Tel: 01752 202301, Fax: 01752 202333
Email: orders@nbninternational.com

IEA subscriptions

The IEA also offers a subscription service to its publications. For a single annual payment (currently £42.00 in the UK), subscribers receive every monograph the IEA publishes. For more information please contact:

Clare Rusbridge
Subscriptions
IEA
2 Lord North Street
FREEPOST LON10168
London SW1P 3YZ
Tel: 020 7799 8907, Fax: 020 7799 2137
Email: crusbridge@iea.org.uk